LOVE YOUR SPIRITUAL GIFTS

By
SUSAN GRAYSON

Published by

Sonoran Mystic Publishing, LLC

Copyright © 2023 by Susan Grayson

All rights reserved.

No portion of this book may be reproduced in any form without written permission from the publisher or author, except as permitted by U.S. copyright law.

This publication is designed to provide accurate and authoritative information in regard to the subject matter covered. It is sold with the understanding that neither the author nor the publisher is engaged in rendering legal, investment, accounting or other professional services. While the publisher and author have used their best efforts in preparing this book, they make no representations or warranties with respect to the accuracy or completeness of the contents of this book and specifically disclaim any implied warranties of merchantability or fitness for a particular purpose. No warranty may be created or extended by sales representatives or written sales materials. The advice and strategies contained herein may not be suitable for your situation. You should consult with a professional when appropriate. Neither the publisher nor the author shall be liable for any loss of profit or any other commercial damages, including but not limited to special, incidental, consequential, personal, or other damages.

ISBN: 979-8-9900246-2-5

Book Cover by Susan Grayson

Illustrations by Susan Grayson

Published by Sonoran Mystic Publishing

Second Edition 2024

Table of Contents

About the Author ii
Dedication ii
Introduction iii
   Chapter One: Growing Spiritually 1
   Chapter Two: The Tarot and My Personal Journey 4
   Chapter Three: The Tarot 7
   Chapter Four: My Move to Corpus Christi, Texas 39
   Chapter Five: Pendulum Magick History 43
   Chapter Six: Psychic Protection 52
   Chapter Seven: Psychometry 62
   Chapter Eight: Candle Magick 65
   Chapter Nine: Scrying 71
   Chapter Ten: Automatic Writing 73
   Chapter Eleven: Past Life Regression 75
   Chapter Twelve: The Study of Wicca 88
   Chapter Thirteen: Meditation 98
   Chapter Fourteen: Chakras 103
   Chapter Fifteen: Auras 107
   Chapter Sixteen: Dreams 109
   Chapter Seventeen: Developing Your Intuition 111
   Chapter Eighteen: Mediumship 114
   Chapter Nineteen: Mediumship Practices 119
   Chapter Twenty: Spirit Help in Connecting With the Other Side 128
   Chapter Twenty-One: Healing 133
   Chapter Twenty-Two: Susan Marie 135
   Chapter Twenty-Three: Pets 140
   Chapter Twenty-Four: Living Your Best Life 143
   Chapter Twenty-Five: How to Live a Meaningful Life Make Peace with Your Past 146
   Chapter Twenty-Six: Growing Up Catholic 151
   Chapter Twenty-Seven: Relationships 153
   Chapter Twenty-Eight: Angels 158

About the Author

As a medium, psychic, teacher, spiritual advisor and published author, Susan Grayson has helped countless people with her intuitive and mediumship skills. She is committed to helping people develop their psychic and spiritual gifts as well as helping them transform the quality of their lives. She shares her experiences and knowledge for the purpose of teaching people about the spiritual world and how to connect to their loved ones on the other side.

Susan has appeared on radio and television, as well as social media demonstrating her gifts. She currently resides in Phoenix, Arizona with her husband.

Susan's website is: www.SusanGraysonPsychicMedium.com

Follow Susan on Facebook at www.facebook.com/susangraysonpsychic

Dedication

To my husband Bill, who has supported me and traveled with me on this spiritual journey. You have taught me the meaning of true love.

To my loving children Juan and Susan Marie, who have made my life so special and so meaningful; I love you both so much!

A special thanks to my creative son, Juan, for all for all of his support and editing my first edition, designing my book cover and business cards.

I lovingly thank my family, friends, teachers and clients who have supported me along the way.

I also would like to thank Don Rumer-Rivera for all the time and toil spent while bringing this book to life and for his constant support with growing and nurturing my business.

And, last of all, I wish to thank my angels, guides and loved ones on the other side who made all this possible.

Introduction

You are a beautiful being of light and one of God's creations. The spiritual gift you have received in this lifetime is that small inner voice, your inner guidance. Learning to pay attention to it will make your journey smoother. Being spiritual is all about paying attention to your feelings and trusting them. It's not about what you know or think you know but how you feel about what's happening within and around you.

This book teaches you how to enlist help from the other side, either with your angels, spiritual guides, or loved ones. We are never alone and loved by God and many in spirit. Your life has meaning, and you are here to fulfill your purpose. You are not here by coincidence or by accident, and your journey was carefully planned and carefully orchestrated before you came here. Every experience and every obstacle is there to help you to grow spiritually and keep you on your path. We chose to be here and to take this journey.

Regardless of your upbringing, and in most circumstances; your teachers, your parents, your friends, your religions, and your societies, they have all done their best to conform you, to brainwash you, to train you and to mold you. Their job has been to control you and to have you think like a responsible member of society. For most of your life, you have not been encouraged to question things or express what has been negatively taught to you. It has all been about going along and living your life in the way that has been expected of you.

I have given you the tools and techniques to develop your spiritual gifts in this book. Some of these tools you may resonate with, while others you may not, but they are here to explore. Many tools are available to you, and I have mentioned the ones to you that I have found most valuable and helpful to me. You are a unique individual, and it is important for you to learn to love yourself and appreciate who you are and all that you are. You are precious and sacred, and it is time to know and use your spiritual gifts so that you may live the best life possible!

I believe our physical bodies may die, but our souls and all the earthly experiences we have had stay with us always. Our personalities will remain with us also.
I have had many visitations in my dreams with my loved ones that have passed over. They have assured me that they are well, happy, and healing on the other side. My loved ones also expressed how their loved ones, relatives, family, friends, and pets were there to welcome them when they passed over.

I had an interesting experience with my cousin Lee when she passed. She and I grew up together, and although we were quite different, we did have some great times and made happy memories together. At the age of 18, Lee went into the army. It was a perfect choice for her because she lacked direction then. When she retired, she was a sergeant major, the highest rank she could achieve. During her life, she suffered from depression and had a nervous breakdown at one point. She also had some addictions, such as gambling, drinking, and chain-smoking.

When Lee retired, she moved to Albuquerque, New Mexico. She, my Aunt Dot, and I would spend a great deal of time together. My cousin was strong and a fighter, and in the years before she died, she developed COPD but would not give up her cigarettes or her other addictions. She was very stubborn.

In her 60s, she was living in an assisted living home. My aunt and I spent a great deal of time visiting her in her final days. She absolutely loved Barbra Streisand and Judy Garland and had their portraits on her walls. She also had an enormous collection of ceramic clowns in a glass case. Lee also loved beautiful gold jewelry.

After Lee died, my Aunt Dot asked me if I wanted any of Lee's jewelry. I said yes, and I took a pair of her gold earrings and a small pinkie ring with an emerald stone.

Shortly after Lee had passed, my Aunt Dot and I spent a day at the spa. As soon as we walked into the spa, facing us on the magazine rack was a magazine with Barbra Streisand's face on the cover. That was unusual because Barbra Streisand had not been in magazines for many years.

Then one day, my aunt and I went to Barnes & Noble and sat down for a drink, and had a conversation about Lee. As we were talking about Lee, my pinky ring gently grazed my purse and the emerald stone contained within the gold setting crumbled into hundreds of tiny specks. We looked at each other in shock. We knew my cousin Lee did that from the other side to let us know she was around us.

It is important that we be aware of the signs that our loved ones send us. They want to be acknowledged and watch over us often. Even though our loved ones may not express themselves as dramatically as Lee did, they are still around us. Our loved ones would appreciate a prayer or thoughts of love sent to them occasionally.

I hope in your life, you choose love instead of fear in your daily activities and that you find that living your life is all worthwhile. I also hope this book helps you on your journey here and that you find magick and miracles along the way.

Much love and many blessings, Susan Grayson

Chapter One: Growing Spiritually

To grow spiritually, you need to be aware of the energy within and around you. Everything is energy. Our own personal vibration is our personal energy. Because we are all individuals and unique, we know what raises our vibrations and what lowers them. We know this by being aware of how this makes us feel.

Let us discuss the things that lower and raise our energy and vibrations. Examples of things that lower our vibration and energy would be:

- Being tired and not getting enough rest or sleep.

- Toxic environments such as littered streets, congested traffic, pollution, condemned buildings and homes, homeless people or camps, dirty, smoky environments, disorganization around you, and any unpleasant sights to look at.

- Seeing animals or people being abused.

- Anger, jealousy, resentment.

- People that drain you and leave you exhausted when in their presence.

- Negative people and uncleanliness.

- Wasting your time doing things you do not want to do.

- Arguing and yelling and expending unnecessary energy.

- Clinging to unhappy memories or sad situations you could not improve.

- Bad relationships or being around people you cannot trust.

- Too much food, too much alcohol, too much worrying, and too much anxiety.

- Working too much and playing too little; your life is out of balance.
- Watching the news.
- Reading depressing and sad stories.
- Listening to people argue and debate on TV.
- Watching programs that show violence.
- Participating in violent games.
- Being around violent people or dangerous situations.
- Feeling helpless and lonely.

Now, let us talk about what raises our vibrations and gives us good energy. Examples are:

- Loving and grounding yourself.
- Laughing and smiling.
- Doing creative things in the arts and being enthusiastic about what you are doing.
- Reading an enjoyable book.
- Walking along the beach and smelling the fresh salt air.
- Walking in nature, seeing the trees, birds, and animals, and looking at the beautiful clouds and sky above you.
- Playing with your pets.
- Playing with children.

- Breathing deeply and focusing on your breathing.

- Meditation, yoga, dancing, music, playing an instrument, painting a picture, doing photography, and writing.

- Riding a horse.

- Amusement rides.

- Eating healthy foods or eating foods you enjoy.

- Sunshine.

- Just Relaxing.

- Watching a good movie.

- Being around people who are supportive because they have your back and your best interest in mind.

- Doing volunteer work and helping others.

- Burning a candle, smelling your favorite oil, taking a luxurious bath with bubbles.

- Being around a garden and smelling the flowers while breathing in the fresh air and fragrant scents.

- Having an adventure.

- Traveling to unfamiliar places.

Chapter Two: The Tarot and My Personal Journey

The Tarot turned my life from ordinary to extraordinary. It opened a whole new world up to me, and it brought gifts into my life that I never could have imagined. As I learned to develop my psychic gifts, everything in my life changed for the better, and it was never the same again. I began to look at life differently, and in doing so, my friends changed. If they were not open to all these new ways of thinking and the metaphysical world, I would have to leave them behind. I was rapidly growing in learning and had this insatiable desire to learn more. I was unstoppable in my pursuit of the new-age literature out there, and I could not get enough!

It was in the early 1980s, and my children were toddlers. My husband and I had just returned from living in Denver, and we were back in our house in Albuquerque. I had this neighbor, Pat, who lived across the street from me and little did I know then, how her friendship would transform my life in incredible and wondrous ways! She was indeed the angel sent to me who would set me on my spiritual path, and I am so grateful for her friendship. I will always love her and appreciate the magick she brought into my life. She was about 30 years older than me and was such an incredible person. One day, she came to my house and brought a set of tarot cards. That was it! I was immediately taken in by this magickal deck of cards. I resonated with the cards and was fascinated by them. She also brought me several books to read, and one of them was on reincarnation. When I read the book on reincarnation, it made so much sense to me. All the answers and theories I had been looking for about life and death were contained in that book. Pat was instrumental in opening my mind to new and interesting ideas and beliefs.

The mystical side of life has always intrigued me. Pat and I spent many hours and days looking in different metaphysical stores at books, tarot cards, and different tools to develop your psychic gifts. It was a world of fascination to me, and I loved it!

As I spent many hours a day working with the Tarot cards and reading the New Age books, I found myself developing my psychic gifts faster than ever before. When I worked with the tarot decks, I would use the protective light around me and connect to the other side with my angels, my spiritual guides, and my God.

At the time, there were many New Age stores in town, and I worked at a few of them, giving readings to clients. I found when I gave readings, messages would come through from the other side. Sometimes, the messages came through as visions of what was going on in the client's lives, and other times, the messages were from the client's loved ones who had passed over.
This was amazing to me, and I knew that the answers I received were true. I could not make these answers up as they came to me from the other side.

I also found that meditation every day helped me connect with the beings on the other side. When I was open to the other side in a beautiful, protected way, what I needed to know would come to me. My whole purpose in doing the readings was to help myself and to help others. I had found my purpose in life, my purpose for being here. When I could help someone, it made me feel good.

Of course, with my strict Boston Irish Catholic background, I had a lot of opposition around me, particularly with family and some friends. My husband, growing up in the Catholic faith also, did not understand all these new age beliefs and was a bit opposed to all of this. So, it was a challenge to believe in myself and in the things that I felt were right when I knew people around me strongly disagreed. But to me, it all felt right deep within me, and I had to keep growing and learning, regardless of what other people believed or how they felt about me and what I was doing. I was being judged as a heathen and criticized by many. But I knew I had to pursue this no matter what, and I knew it was to help others with their lives. I could help counsel people in a spiritual way and to help them believe in themselves. I could also help them understand that although they were in the world, they were not of the world. That they were a spiritual body having a physical experience here on earth.

I practiced with my cards and meditated diligently. I attended many psychic fairs in Albuquerque and the El Paso fairs five times a year. I knew what I was doing was right for me, and regardless of the changes ahead of me, I had to go on with it. I found my purpose in life, and it made sense now more than ever before.

In 1986, in January, I went back to school and finished my degree in art education. It was important to get a degree and get a regular job. In 1990, I got a job teaching art in Tucumcari, New Mexico. As much as I enjoyed teaching art, it was not enough to fulfill my dreams. The art world was beautiful and creative, with so many choices to choose from, but it did not thrill me like the new age studies did. Teaching art was a way to make a living, but it did not fill the void within me.

During that time, my husband and I divorced because I felt like I was still growing and we were taking different paths in life. He was not interested in the metaphysical path I had chosen. However, I will always be grateful to my husband for the two beautiful children we had together and the 14 years we spent raising them. I absolutely loved his parents and his family, too. But I was a driven woman who had to change my life and follow my path.

After my husband and I divorced, I remarried and got a job teaching special education in Gallup, New Mexico. I taught for two years in Gallup, then moved back to Albuquerque and pursued my metaphysical studies by teaching classes in metaphysics and doing readings full-time. I continued doing psychic fairs, which were extremely popular back then.

Chapter Three: The Tarot

The Tarot and its History

The origin of the Tarot remains a mystery. Some people believe that the tarot deck dates to Egyptian and Sumerian civilizations, symbolizing the secret teachings of their religions. Others believe that the tarot was brought to Europe by fortune telling gypsies coming from either Egypt or India. Other theories suggest the tarot originated in China. No matter the truth, the cards were widely used in Italy, France, and Germany by the late 14th century. The oldest existing version is dated around 1390.

The tarot cards may not have been used for cartomancy or divination purposes until the end of the 16th century or the beginning of the 17th century.

Because the Tarot was used for divination purposes, it suggests they were once considered "holy." The word divination comes from the word divine, meaning lofty, celestial, Godly and heavenly.

The word Tarot comes from Taro-Rota, which means the will of the law and the law of the will. The French used the Tarot in the 18th century, which is why the final t in Tarot is silent.

The Tarot and How to Work with Your Tarot Cards

For the Tarot, I have chosen the Ryder Waite Tarot deck because it is traditional and because of all the symbols and illustrations on each card.
I have been working with tarot cards for over 40 years, and I have never stopped learning about them. They are truly a fascinating tool for divination. There are so many books on tarot out on the market and hundreds of tarot decks to choose from. I have spent countless hours working with them.

The tarot is an ancient tool and is a divination, a ritual, a ceremonial act, a magickal action, and a way to meditate. Because it is a divination tool, meaning "from the divine," it implies that we are communicating with higher intelligence or beings.

The tarot tells a story that relates to your life in some way. The cards tell you of the past, present, and future. The tarot gives you the opportunity to widen your perspective and will help you increase your intuitive abilities.

In first learning the tarot, I would suggest buying a traditional tarot deck and when you feel comfortable that you know the cards, symbolism, meanings, and definitions well, then, buy a deck that you strongly resonate with.

Traditional decks would be any of the Ryder Waites, Hanson Roberts, Robin Wood, Gilded Tarot, or Morgan Greer.

Oracle decks differ from the tarot because they usually have fewer cards and pertain to a subject, such as dolphins, angels, fairies, etc.

Once you have purchased your deck, you would want to cleanse, purify, and put your own energy into it. You may do this by burying them in sea salt, burning sage or incense around them, placing them in a plastic bag and putting them in the freezer, or running them over a burning candle. This helps remove any previous energy that may be negative from other people or environments. By cleansing your cards you are making their energy clear, and now you can put your energy into them.

After cleansing your cards, place them in a special pouch, cloth, box, or container. If you allow people to handle your cards, always shuffle them seven times after they have handled them to clear the energy on them. By shuffling them seven times this will remove any existing patterns and energy according to the principles of mathematical randomization. You may want to keep your tarot deck stored with stones and crystals or any little objects that are significant to you.
To get acquainted with your cards, you may meditate with them, sleep with them, or carry them with you wherever you go.

You can practice with your cards by doing a spread daily, or you can practice in the evening before going to bed. Shuffle your cards, then fan out the cards face down and, randomly choose one, and meditate on it. You will know what card to choose because the energy will feel different, or you may feel drawn to that card. Then, place that card under your pillow and go to sleep. You may just have some very prophetic dream or awaken with a truly clear understanding of the meaning of that card. The more you work with your cards, the more they will work for you.

The Tarot Deck and the Major Arcana

The traditional Tarot deck contains seventy-eight cards. Twenty-two are the major arcana, and fifty-six are the minor Arcana.

The major cards represent the spiritual laws of metaphysical growth, and they are the main lessons to be learned. They represent our actual personalities, show us the way, and show us our deepest secrets.

The minor cards help us define and clarify the story of the major arcana. They are divided into four suits. The suits are wands, cups, swords, and pentacles.

The tarot is also like a journey that the fool goes on through his life. It is divided into three phases: adolescence, lessons learned, and achievements from successes.

ADOLESCENCE

- FOOL- Traveler on the tarot path. Starting out on a journey with hope and enthusiasm.

- MAGICIAN- Teacher, mentor, educator to the fool.

- EMPRESS- Mortal Earth mother.

- EMPEROR- Mortal earth father.

- HIGH PRIESTESS- Celestial, spiritual mother.

- HIEROPHANT- Celestial, spiritual father.

- LOVERS - Experiencing love and the relationships in the fool's life.

- CHARIOT- Conflicts and struggles in the fool's life and his ability to keep moving forward and staying on his spiritual path.

LESSONS LEARNED

- JUSTICE- Clear thinking, balancing his mind, being impartial, and learning how to look at both sides of a situation without judgment.

- TEMPERANCE- Cooperation, balancing his heart and emotions. He is also learning patience and trying to maintain peace of mind.

- STRENGTH- He is learning courage and fortitude as well as perseverance.

- HERMIT- Learning self-discipline and the importance of time and meditation. He is also taking the time to find and know himself. He is learning to look inward for answers and find his truth.

- WHEEL OF FORTUNE- The fool is facing many unpredictable changes in his life and adjusting to the difficulties and challenges confronting him.

- HANGED MAN- A time for sacrificing and a turning point in his conscious and unconscious mind. He is finding things are going slower than he wants them to. He may be feeling frustrated and stuck.

ACHIEVEMENTS

- DEATH- This is a time for him of rebirth, transformation, and stripping of all pretensions. The old dies away, and the new is born. This is a new chapter in the fool's life.

- DEVIL- This is a time for the fool to face his own shadow and darkness and move beyond his fears.

- TOWER- This is the card of divine intervention, a time for the fool to have to start all over again and rebuild his life. It is a wake-up call, and his life will never be the same again, but after rebuilding it, it will be better.

- STAR- This card brings hope, inspiration, and reawakening into the fool's life once again. This is the light at the end of the tunnel.

- MOON- This is a time in the fool's life that is full of fluctuation and change. His unconscious mind, vivid dreams, inner knowing, and intuition are important right now. He must learn to trust his inner guidance.

- SUN- This is the happiest card in the tarot deck. It indicates triumphs, light, perception, victory, success, directness, and enjoyment.

- JUDGEMENT- This card indicates the fool's success and achievements, as well as peace of mind after many struggles.

- WORLD- This is a time for the fool to sit back and enjoy the fruits of his labor, and all his successes, and what he has attained. It is also a time for him to make new plans and set new goals for his future.

Major Arcana Meanings

0 FOOL

On this tarot card, the Sun is bright with promises of the future. The youth is looking out into the distance instead of his feet. The white rose represents his spiritual desires, which are innocent and pure. The red feather in his hat represents the color of his physical desires. The white dog is a symbol of God in natural creatures, who is playful and gives us unconditional love.

Because the fool stands at the edge of the precipice, he is prepared to take the leap into unknown territory.

The fool is often shown in the cards at the crossroads because he must make the choice of where to go. He is full of energy, and he follows his path with faith. He is innocent, trusting, and is willing to take risks as he makes his journey. He is like a child discovering life for the first time.

In a reading, this card can mean you are beginning a new chapter in your life. It could indicate an adult searching for a new opportunity, an adventure, or an escape. Sometimes, this card indicates the person needs to have more fun and be more childlike, or it could be the opposite, which means they are having too much fun and need to settle down, get more serious, and show responsibility

1 MAGICIAN

The Magician wears the white robe, which represents inner purity and innocence, and the red cloak, which represents purposeful activity and courage. The lemniscate over his head represents the symbol of eternal life and dominion. The white lilies are pure abstract thoughts representing the spiritual world, while the red roses represent the physical world and our physical thoughts.

The four elements on the table represent fire, earth, water, and air, and they are also the four functions of consciousness which are intuition which is wands, sensation which is earth, feelings which are cups, and thinking which are swords. The columns supporting the table indicate the need to rise above to the spiritual world which is above the physical world.

The Magician has an attitude of power and command, and he holds his wand high as he receives from the spiritual plane. He is a conscious link between man and spirit, teacher, or guide. The Magician offers education and enlightenment, revealing the fool's potential and possibilities in life.

The Magician teaches us that everything is possible through the power of God. He indicates an important beginning, a time for action. He teaches the fool that the resources that one possesses are not limited to their physical capabilities.

In a reading, this card tells us that there are powers from heaven and earth available to everyone; by combining both, one can manifest his dreams.

2 HIGH PRIESTESS

She represents unseen wisdom. The curtain behind her is the tree of life. The scrolls she holds are the Torah, which represents divine law and is a secret document of wisdom and hidden mysteries. The two pillars are the division of dimensions between illusion and reality, conscious and unconscious mind, male and female, and the positive and negative life force.

Solomon's temple is represented by two pillars: the J for Jachin, which represents positive energy, and the B for Boaz, which represents negative energy. The vertical part of the cross represents the male, and the horizontal part represents the female. The palms represent the male, while the pomegranates represent the female. She represents stillness, withdrawal, and intuitive awareness.

The high priestess teaches the fool the power of his inner guidance. Her wisdom gives balance coming from dreams and meditations. She is free from emotional or physical attachment. She is the keeper of secrets, intuitiveness, spirituality, wisdom, meditation, and balance. She teaches the fool to focus inward for his solutions.

In a reading, this card is connected to the occult, spiritual ideas, esoteric matters, development of intuition, and natural insight. The high priestess teaches that you have the answers within you.

3 EMPRESS

The empress represents abundance. She wears a necklace, which is the pearl of wisdom, and she sits in a fertile garden surrounded by ripening wheat. There is a stream which is the water of life, giving life to all. The scepter she holds with the world globe is her domination over the created world. She wears a crown with twelve signs of the zodiac. The heart-shaped stone near her feet is Venus, or the symbol of woman, and the number three is the number of harmony and things coming together.

She is the promise of growth, prosperity, and fertility in all things. She has compassion and tolerance. She teaches you to ground your energies and tells you to use a passionate approach instead of an intellectual one. She represents growth, healing, and fruitfulness.

The empress teaches the fool to care for himself and his body. She is the fool's earth mother who loves and feels compassion for all creatures of the earth. She represents protection and preservation.

In a reading, this card represents love of all kinds. She also represents happy, stable relationships, marriage, or motherhood. She can also indicate a child is on the way. It is a good card to get if you are contemplating marriage. She exemplifies all the love we seek, self-love, individual love, love of nature, family love, or a lover. She is the goddess of love, harmony, and beauty. She also indicates that there may be an abundance coming to the client.

4 EMPEROR

The emperor is all about discipline and the law. The ankh is the Egyptian symbol of life, vitality, and victory. The ram head represents the emblem of Mars. The number four represents stability. The globe has dominion, and the cubic throne is its anchor in the physical world.

The emperor is the Lord of thought, unbending in his judgment, indicated by his stern, regal posture and masculine energy. He is the fool's earth father, and he takes responsibility, is courageous, and a good leader. He is ambitious, facing decisions that require assertiveness and insensitivity.

This emperor may represent issues with one's father, brother, son, or husband. He teaches the fool about reaching goals with intellect and reason, and how to manage the material side of life.

In a reading, this card represents the drive through ambition, power, wealth, and fame. It represents the power of organization, putting order in one's life. The emperor represents balance, authority, and mind over matter, experience, knowledge, and discipline.

5 HIEROPHANT

This is the card of the high priest of religion or tradition. The triple crown he wears is of a pope, three layers rules over the creative, formative, and material world. The two students are seekers of higher ideals. The number five represents mental inspiration and creative thought.
The two pillars represent duality. The cross keys are the keys of the kingdom. The gold represents the sun and the superconscious mind, and the silver is the moon and the subconscious mind.

The hierophant is the teacher, the educator, the one who stimulates inner awakening in the fool. He also represents religious ideas and the search for truth. He is a link between God and man, spirit and matter.

He is the fool's spiritual father and represents moral law and the accepted code of behavior within society. He gives the fool guidance on spiritual matters and the need for the fool to find spiritual meaning in his life.

In a reading, this card teaches you to have faith in the higher powers, laws, and ideals and that intuitive guidance is the way to self-fulfillment.

6 LOVERS

Lovers represent the fool's emotional life and his choices. The palms are open, which represents new possibilities in a relationship. Archangel Raphael is the angel of air, giving blessings. The serpent represents eternal life. The man is the conscious mind and reason, while the woman represents the subconscious mind and emotions. The angel represents the superconscious mind. Number six is about cooperation and marriage.

In a reading, this card represents all relationship choices. This card is the coming together of opposites. The fool is learning to recognize sides of himself he has refused to acknowledge in the past. It can represent partners reuniting. This card is also about magnetism and attraction and about allowing love and beauty into your life. The fool is learning how to develop communication with another person and realizing it is time to make a choice regarding relationships.

7 CHARIOT

The chariot represents magick, movement, and control. The wand represents authority to control and manage the sphinxes. The white sphinx represents mercy and positive life principles. The black sphinx represents stern justice and negative life principles.

The prince maintains a balance between them. The Hindu sign in front is the union of male and female. There are wings of spirit over the Hindu sign.

The fool is learning the importance of exercising self-discipline, directing himself wisely, being focused, and the ability to regulate his life.

This card is about releasing emotions. With continued effort the fool can win and be triumphant. He needs to use his talents and energy constructively for a purpose. Progress through balancing opposing forces. Number seven represents seven planets, seven virtues, seven vices, seven ages of man, seven days of the week, seven seals in the book of revelations.

In a reading, this card represents movement, self-control, and self-discipline. Finding the balance between aggressive and passive actions. It is about taking control and doing what you really want. It can also indicate traveling soon, moving through all obstacles. It is about victory, and the energy needed to fight for the desired goal.

8 STRENGTH

This card represents inner vitality and courage to face challenges. The fool is learning that the inner qualities of love and patience are superior to hate and negativity. Number eight is the symbol of eternity and balance, as each loop is the same. The lion represents strong passion, and the white dress represents purity. The strength is well-centered, has self-respect, and possesses earned confidence.

The strength card teaches us that brute force is never a match for spiritual strength. This card is about inner fortitude, will, and determination. One should use perseverance to overcome adversity.

In a reading, this card may indicate that someone will overcome illness. If your client has a question about health and gets the strength card, it usually indicates good health and healing to come.

9 HERMIT

The hermit is all about inner wisdom and teaching by example. Ask, and it shall be given.
He represents the search for spiritual enlightenment. The lantern represents the lamp of truth. The six-pointed star represents radiant energy. The hermit represents the fool who arrives at the mountaintop, which is a high point of spiritual wisdom.

The hermit is about introspection, meditation, and the search for inner knowledge. Time alone may be necessary to re-create harmony and order in one's life. It may mean withdrawing from active life for a while. This card is concerned with the truth and what is real. It is about soul-searching and meditation.

In a reading, this card may indicate a need for the client to spend time alone to work things out quietly. Or it may indicate that the person has a need for socialization and has been spending too much time alone.

10 WHEEL OF FORTUNE

The Wheel of Fortune talks about change and a turn of events. It is represented with the mystical animals from the Bible Ezekiel 1:10 revelation 4:7. The animals represent the four fixed signs of the zodiac. The bull, which is Taurus, meaning earth; the lion, which is Leo, meaning fire; the eagle which is Scorpio, meaning water; and the man or angel which is Aquarius, meaning air.

The jackal is Anubis, the Egyptian God, and is a conductor of souls. The snake is the Egyptian God, Set, who brought death to the world. The sphinx is resurrection, life triumphant over death. Taro means tarot, and IHVH is Jehovah.

The symbols on the inner circle are the alchemical symbols, which stand for mercury, sulfur, water, and salt.

This fool is learning that life is constantly changing and is always in the process of mystery and wonder. What is here today could be gone tomorrow. When he is down on the wheel, the only way to go is up. Spiritual reality is unchanging, although personal life turns and changes.
Opportunities come and go. He can turn a negative into a positive, and everything passes unexpectedly.

In a reading, this card could represent a sudden change of fortune, good or bad. This is a new phase in life. A new chapter is starting, and important decisions are to be made. A new run of luck may be commencing. The more you are aware of your power over your destiny, the clearer things will appear. You need to be centered, heal, and have faith and trust.

11 JUSTICE

Justice represents truth. The pillars are positive and negative. The eyes are open to see all that is going on. The scales represent balanced judgment. The sword is double-edged and cuts two ways, indicating action. This card is about restoring balance and harmony in the world with fairness. It indicates the need for a balanced mind and that problems must be solved impartially with fairness and reason. The sword cuts away ignorance, and the scales weigh experiences. It is time to consider both sides. As you sow, so shall you reap. Now is the time for cutting away unnecessary baggage.

In a reading, this card could be about arriving at a decision that is fair and honest. Looking honestly at our lives and seeing the truth. One may need to develop better health habits and take responsibility for one's actions. This card could also indicate some legal matters.

12 HANGED MAN

The hanged man teaches the fool about sacrificing and releasing. The man's legs form a cross. The nimbus around the head is sacrificing the ego for the spiritual. The face expresses deep entrancement, not suffering, and that existing conditions may have to be endured for a while longer. Changing the way we see things or changing our lives for the better. Overcoming obstacles through patience and contemplation. Possibly giving up old attitudes and beliefs. There may be postponed plans. Something may need to be sacrificed to acquire something of greater value. This may be a time of greater understanding.
In a reading, it may mean it is a time to relax and to look at things differently. It could mean a spiritual breakthrough and learning to let go. It can be a time of frustration because everything feels like it is in limbo, stuck, and not moving forward.

13 DEATH

Death teaches the fool all about change and transitions in life. It is about death and rebirth. The sun of immortality is between the two towers. The river is the constant flow to the sea, up to the clouds, to the rivers, and to the streams. The fool learns that there must be death for there to be birth. This can be the death of the old self, change, transformation, rebirth, and rejuvenation. As depicted, death rides over everyone, regardless of their status. This card is about learning the value of letting go and moving from one point of life to the next. It is about recognizing the necessity of endings and clearing away rubbish from the past.

In a reading, this card is the inevitable ending of something, but with a promise of a new beginning. It can be loss, change, and renewal. We cannot resist sudden changes; it is necessary for our spiritual growth. This can also be the end of old relationships.

14 TEMPERANCE

The fool is learning all about patience, balance and moderation. The sun is on the forehead of Archangel Michael, and the crown is above the mountain pass, meaning the crown of attainment and mastery. The two peaks represent wisdom and understanding and the union of male and female. Archangel Michael is pouring the essence of life from the silver cup (which is the subconscious mind) to the gold cup (which is the conscious mind). This action means from spirit into matter, passing through the present and into the future. The triangle in the square represents spirit. The balance is the foot on land and water, meaning the spirit (water) and the material (land). The fool can be experiencing adaptability to new environments.

In a reading, this card can mean balancing all elements in your life. And when this action is taken, there is peace and harmony to come. It may mean to use moderation in all things. It may be telling the client that they have learned past lessons well. Temperance has the qualities of compassion and forgiveness, balanced emotions, and cooperation.

15 DEVIL

The devil is all about materialism and teaching the fool to deal with his fears. The devil represents the sensory side of life. The chains around the neck of the couple can easily be lifted. They are chained to the devil through their thoughts and fears. The horned-hooved devil is Pan, the Greek God worshiped by the Greeks as a life-giving fertility god, abundant in procreation. The devil's right hand is raised in the sign of Black Magick. The left-hand holds an inverted flaming torch of destruction. The inverted pentagram represents evil intent.

In a reading, this card represents difficulties caused by the demands and needs of the physical world. It tells us to lighten up and break old habits. It also tells us we are too wrapped up in material concerns. This is about choosing the path of good or evil. It teaches that we can be chained to our fears and that the lessons in life are never-ending. We may be tied to people or situations that are not good for us. The devil could indicate that your possessions are possessing you. The devil is created out of our fears.

16 TOWER

The tower is the card of our destruction, our fall. The tower teaches the fool that it is time to allow everything to fall apart and to rebuild it all over again. The tower represents material ambition, and the fool needs to balance his physical world with the spiritual world. Lightning is the righteous spirit that awakens him.

It is a sudden glimpse of truth shown in the lightning, the flash of inspiration, breakthrough, quick and forceful change. It is a change of values, lifestyle, or location, broken homes, friendships, etc. It is a necessary loss of some kind. It is about tearing down and starting over by breaking down existing forms to make way for new ones. The tower is the defeat of false philosophies and the triumph of true ones. It can be the end of previous patterns, leading to new beginnings.

In a reading, the tower is all about cleaning houses and being made humble. It tells us to be prepared because a situation will change rapidly. This is the time to take a good, long look at your life because, in a catastrophic way, your life will never be the same. This is a necessary change because you have been living too much of a material existence. Spiritual truth breaks down our ignorance. Take a good, long look at your life and be prepared because a situation will change rapidly.

17 STAR

This is the card of good health, hope, and aspirations. It shows balance because one knee is on land, and a foot is on water. The bird is represented by Ibis, the sacred bird of thought, resting in the trees of the mind. The eight stars are the radiant energy of the cosmos. The pool of water is our universal consciousness, and the earth is the matter. The star teaches the fool about having hope and believing in the accomplishments of his goals presently being developed. It is the light at the end of the tunnel. This is a card of meditation telling us that if we listen, the truth will unveil itself.

In a reading, this card teaches the fool about the return of hope, inspiration, and radiant energy. That our visions and dreams will become a reality. The inspiration is from above. It is a happy promise, good fortune, optimism, and joy.

18 MOON

This card is all about intuition and our inner guidance. The crab is ruled by the moon and crawls out of the water to a higher conscious unfoldment. The wolf is the untamed animal, whereas the dog has adapted to man's life. The path leads us to higher consciousness. The towers in the background represent good and evil, negative and positive, the conscious and unconscious minds.
The moon is represented by the high priestess, the goddess, keeper of the mysteries of the universe and she cries tears which fertilize the land. The pond is stagnant and represents our past. This can be a period of confusion, fluctuation, and uncertainty. It is about our intuition and our imagination.

In a reading, it tells the fool to pay attention and believe in his dreams and visions. There is nothing to fear except fear itself. The moon asks us to listen to our inner voice for true direction. Answers are to be found through our dreams and intuitions rather than logic and reason. Pay attention to what your body is telling you. You may be feeling pulled to some purpose. Allow your intuitive powers to guide you.

19 SUN

The child is riding without a saddle because he represents a perfect balance in control between the conscious minds. The flowers are the cultivated garden of men. The four sunflowers represent the four elements: air, fire, water, and earth. It is number 19 because that is the age of initiation.

The sun gives warmth and life to the earth; it is spiritual energy and the protective God. The four sunflowers also represent the four kingdoms: mineral, vegetable, animal, and human. The child brings new life, joy, and inspiration. This is about being open and following one's path. That there is joy and happiness in your future. It represents material wealth, good health, and optimism.

In a reading, this card is the omen of good things to come. This is the happiest card in the major arcana. It is the realization of hopes, dreams, and efforts. This card teaches the fool about enlightenment and understanding, the gifts of clarity and wisdom. The sun is about energy and a source of strength, prosperity, and faithful friends.

20 JUDGEMENT

This card is about self-analysis, resurrection, and regeneration. The cross on the banner represents balanced forces. Angel Gabriel blows seven blasts to wake a man from earthly limitations. The coffins represent the body that is in prison until it is liberated at death, and it is floating on the sea of the subconscious mind. The blast from the horn liberates the man. Judgment is about karma and understanding.

This card is the fool clearing away emotions of his past and forgiveness of himself and others. This card frees the fool to move on. It is an awakening of nature under the influence of the spirit and mystery of birth and death. Judgment is about a higher purpose, deeper meaning, and a new sense of me.

In a reading, this card is an awakening and talks about many lessons learned. It tells the client that if they keep their senses open, they will see and hear the truth. It is about looking back at what has been done and making a clear evaluation. It can be the end of a chapter in life, the completion of a karmic cycle and rewards for past efforts. It is atonement and acknowledging you have changed in some way.

21 WORLD

This is the card of victorious completions. There are four animals from the Bible: Ezekiel and Apocalypse. The wreath represents nature and is the symbol of success and triumph. The four zodiac signs are the four seasons and the four elements. The purple sash is the color of wisdom and divinity. The dancer represents the final attainment of man and the blending of all consciousness. She dances the dance of time and eternity.

This card means enjoying the fruits of victory. It is time to relax and have fun. All your needs are provided for, and this is fulfillment. All the things in the world are possible. There could be a new life in a new place. Achievement, success, sense of peace, travel. This is the realization of a sought-after prize or goal. It is about seeing the whole picture. This is a time for joyful participation in the creation of life.

The client should feel free to go in any direction in a reading. It may be time to create or build a new vision for themselves. They will be triumphant in any new undertaking.

The Minor Arcana

The minor arcana pertains to the four suits:

The first suit is represented by Wands. The best word I would use to describe wands is our intuition. The wands represent fire, the direction of the South, and the time of the year: spring. They also represent the three Fire signs in the zodiac: Aries, Sagittarius, and Leo. In playing cards, they represent clubs. The symbol of the leaf on the wand represents living energy, constant renewal of life, spirituality, passion, and the inner fire that burns within us.

The next suit is cups. This card represents feelings. The cups represent water, the direction of West, and the time of the year, summer. They also represent the three water signs in the zodiac: Pisces, Scorpio, and Cancer. In the playing cards, they represent hearts. The cups deal with our emotional matters, love and happiness, sentiments, and the ebb and flow of all emotional states.

The next suit is swords, which represent thinking. They are the element of air, the direction of the East, and the time of the year which is fall. The swords represent the air signs of the zodiac which are Libra, Gemini, and Aquarius. In the playing cards they represent spades. The swords deal with the mind, activity, thoughts, ideas, decisions, mental action, strife and misfortune, quests, ambition, courage, and transformation.

The final suit we will mention is the pentacles, which represent sensations. They are the elements of the earth, the direction of the North, and the time of the year is the winter. They also represent the three earth signs of the zodiac, which are Virgo, Capricorn, and Taurus. In the playing cards, they represent diamonds. Pentacles pertain to the physical world. The pentacles are the things of the earth that can be seen and touched, possessions, physical health, money, interest, material gain, and industry. The five points on the pentacles represent our five senses of men, the five elements of nature, and the five extremities of the body. It also represents earth, air, fire, water, and spirit.

ACES

The aces are number one, which are creative power, potential beginnings, and a tremendous upsurge of power and energy.

The Ace of Wands shows a castle with a promise of what the future might bring. For example: it could be a new business venture, a new undertaking, and it indicates potential and ambition to succeed. It is an awakening spirit and represents insights and breakthroughs. In other words, it represents a new life.

The ace of cups shows a dove on the card, symbolizing spiritual values. There are five streams of water, which are our five senses. The water lily represents emotional growth. The water represents feelings and emotions. This could be the beginning of a new relationship, love, marriage, motherhood, and immense joy gained from a loving union. It also represents abundance in all things and nourishment from spiritual sources. Deep feelings, following the heart. Visions of aspiration, faith, and hope that light will be revealed.

The ace of swords is about the power of intellect and having strength in adversity. It is a two-edged sword that cuts both ways. The crown represents a symbol of material attainment, while the olive branch is a symbol of peace. The palm leaf is victory. The swords represent air and intellect. For example, out of evil, something good will come. Great power, force, and strength. It is the clarity of the mind. Expansion of thoughts. Assessing a situation and making good decisions.

The ace of pentacles is represented by a beautiful, well-cared-for garden, which means a positive reward for arduous work. The pentacle represents earth, body, matter, and material gain. It is about worldly status, achievement, financial Security, and wealth. An example would be good beginnings for financial propositions, business ventures, or enterprises. It indicates prosperity and ecstasy and earthly power and possessions. It talks about a firm financial foundation, windfall, and a helping hand from above.

TWOS

The two represent opposites: positive or negative, male, or female, spirit, or matter. It can also represent duality or balance of forces.

In the wands, twos are opportunities. There are castle walls, and there are two wands firmly planted showing what has been achieved. The globe represents future possibilities. The white lilies represent pure thoughts, while the roses represent physical desires. Both are equal, showing a well-balanced nature. This card could show lofty ideals, a desire for travel, a new outlook, success through strength and vision. It is a message that tells you to follow your inspiration with action.

The two cups show a balance of opposites, love, emotion, and energy. It is mutuality and a happy union. The serpents on the card represent good and evil. The lion represents carnal desire. The wings of the spirit represent a happy balance between spiritual and physical love. It means the beginning of romance or a well-balanced friendship. In a relationship, focus on positive qualities rather than differences in love. It can also be about clarity and understanding of each other in a relationship.

The two swords represent a stalemate, a tense situation, or an impasse. The blindfold on the card indicates they cannot see their way through their present situation. The sea represents our emotions. The jagged rocks are hard facts. The swords will balance for the moment. The meaning of the card is courage and goodwill coming out of a tough situation. There may be indecision and letting things ride. There is a need to balance your heart and mind.

The two pentacles show a person balancing light heartedly, although the sea is rough. The meaning of this card is the difficulties of the future, juggling finances, and a need for flexibility. It is harmony amid change, agility and handling several things at once. It tells you to go with the flow, work, and dance with the situation at hand.

THREES

The three is about growth and expansion: one, meaning the idea; two, the pair who can conduct the idea; and three, the fruit of the partnership and the initial completion.
The three of wands is about the birth of an enterprise and cooperation. The efforts are rewarded in this card. It also can mean help from a third party. It is about integrity, alignment of energy and feelings that bring about powerful action.

The three of cups are about celebration, having fun, and the time to rejoice. The three of cups tells us to enjoy the moment of celebration. There is abundance and healing to come. It is communion with others. One should guard themselves against taking things too seriously.

The three of swords indicate heartache, necessary cutting away, or a bleeding heart. The stormy weather on the card is about emotions, quarrels, or separation; difficulties in a relationship can be worked out if faced honestly. This card can also indicate a surgery coming up or a broken heart. It talks of delays. This card is about being influenced by past difficulties. Freeing oneself from the past. Heartbreaks and sorrow. A need to create space for healing to occur.

The three of pentacles are about jobs well done and beneficial use of your talents. It is about mastering one's craft, and the sense of achievement. It can mean taking control of a project or stage of development, and skillful action.

FOURS

The fours are about reality, logic, and reason. Mind, body, spirit, and material plane.

The four of wands are a haven of refuge, a well-deserved rest. This is a happy and productive card indicating harmony and union. Stability comes from completing a task. Starting a successful venture. Prosperity and peace at home. Bridging spiritual and physical worlds.

The four of cups indicate discontent. It is a card of boredom, confusion, and being unhappy. There is a need to look at life in a fresh way, a re-assessment. Outer and inner emotional conflicts. Seeing the true value in one's life. See what is being offered instead of what has been.

The four of swords is about respite, recharging your batteries. It is about rest or retreat after a struggle. Quiet time. A time for thinking things through, recuperation period, peace. Allowing destructive ideas to pass away. Remembering life is sacred. A need to retreat and regroup and a need for more clarity.

The four of pentacles is about holding tight, maintaining your status. It is about holding onto something, nothing ventured, nothing gained. It can be about stinginess and power. Defining oneself by possessions or wealth. Practical and realistic methods for attaining physical Security.

FIVES

The fives are about uncertainty, change, shift, and adversity.

The five of wands may indicate battles, or exciting and challenging times. They are the struggles in life and love. Difficulties in communication, competition, opposition, and disagreements.

The five of cups can mean a time of mourning, loss, and disappointment. Maybe having regrets over past actions. A need for movement again. Suppressed anger at losses, delays, and emotional transitions.

The five of swords can be about negative energy, or empty victory. It is about swallowing your pride and accepting your limitations before moving upward and onward. Possibly proceeding in a new direction. You may be in a situation where you are in competition with another.

The five of pentacles speak of poverty and feeling down and out. It can be strain or anxiety over money. Emotionally feeling out in the cold, a feeling of destitution. It may be time to let go of the past. Freedom from restrictions of the past. Taking the bitter lesson that life gives us. It can mean worries or concerns about financial Security or poverty. Also, it can be about abusing the body, such as drugs or other substances.

SIXES

The sixes are about equilibrium, harmony, and balance. The six stars are equal to triangles. One pointing to heaven, and the other one pointing to earth with balance between them.

The sixth of wands is about victory and success. Triumph, achievement, fulfillment of hopes and wishes. Great satisfaction, assurance, and a message from within us as to what direction to take.

The six of cups is about nostalgia, the good old days and focusing too much on the past. It is a card of memories, meetings, or reunions with an old friend or family member. It can mean innocence and sharing in a loving way.

The six of swords is about leaving troubles behind and focusing on brighter days ahead. It is a passage away from difficulties, success after anxiety, and more peaceful days to come. It can mean traveling in the mind or body. New shores are approaching, which could be new opportunities coming your way.

The six of pentacles is a card of generosity and getting what you deserve. There is financial help. The client will receive what is rightfully his. Sharing prosperity with others and the willingness to give and receive. Giving from your heart and not from your ego.

SEVENS

The number seven is about wisdom, completion of cycles such as the seven planets in astrology, the seven virtues, the seven vices, the seven sins, and the seventh day that God rested. It is a loss of stability.

The seven of wands are about holding firm, holding your own, and being in an advantageous position. Strength and determination are necessary to achieve success. Overcoming obstacles and persevering to win. Finding your inner strength and standing up for your beliefs.

The seven of cups can indicate daydreams, lack of focus, and confusion. There are choices to be made. Abundance, creative, artistic talent, and energy. Forces may be scattered. It is about possibilities, fantasies, but watch out for overindulgence.

The seven of swords are talking about stealth and doing the unexpected. It can be a flight from a dishonorable act, deceit, betrayal, thievery, or someone taking advantage of the client. Not all things are being revealed. Need to be honest with oneself and others. A need for research to find out what is really going on.

The seven of pentacles are perseverance, slow and steady growth, taking stock of one's investments. There is consistent effort needed, and the possibility of a delay. Need to get working. Learn from past experiences. Anxiety, fear of satisfaction or completion.

EIGHTS

The eight is about regeneration and balance of opposing forces. Death of the old and making way for new. Unexpected shift.

The eight of cups is leaving emotional situations behind and moving on forward. A time in your life where you no longer want to dwell on the past. Leave the emotional drama behind.

The eight of wands is about speed, acting swiftly, full-steam ahead. This is a time for activities and new beginnings and the end of the period of delay. Exciting time ahead, travel, movement. Lots of ideas are coming in at once, rapid developments. Communication needed. A quick end to a complicated issue

The eight of swords can make you feel trapped or restricted. It is about fear and indecision, restricting oneself, and bondage. You need to be calm and quiet. Really, look carefully at an issue.

The eight of pentacles is about apprenticeship and is a working card. It is about craftsmanship, employment to come, and career. It tells you to be prepared. Learning and creating with your skills. Keeping your books balanced. Knowledge of the workings of the world.

NINES

The nines are all the forces of the other numbers summed up. Forming a foundation before completion.

The nine of wands is about strength and determination. Strength in reserve, victory through courage, endurance, and preparedness. It is about standing your ground, being defensible, and holding off. It can indicate suspicion. Setting boundaries with people.

The nine of cups are your desires and wishes fulfilled. It is a card of well-being, material success, happiness, satisfaction, and Security. It is also about giving birth to a dream.

The nine of swords can be despair, a nightmare, but fear is far worse than the outcome. It is a stressful situation and could be the death of a loved one. Negative thinking, excessive criticism of self. Failure of a plan of action moving from self-judgment to self-acceptance.

The nine of pentacles is about self-reliance and being self-sufficient. It is the kind of material well-being, enjoying the good things in life, and material benefits that are promised and appreciated. It is a card and good luck and good management. Enjoying the harvest. Discrimination in choices and need to be open to abundance to come.

TENS

The ten is the number of perfections through completion. The cups and pentacles indicate the height of bliss and happiness while the swords and wands are about trial and tribulation as well as the final transformation.

The ten of wands are the weights of ambition, and the burdens of success. This is a heavy burden in the load that can be mental, emotional, or physical. The problem will soon be solved. It is about oppression, holding back due to lack of energy or direction. Self-limiting visions of what is possible. Taking responsibility for one's own karma and creations.

The ten of cups are about joy and harmony in personal relationships. This is the card of a happy family life and attainment of your heart's desires. There is love to give and receive. Emotional completion. Blissful feelings and the ability to conduct your plans effectively.

The ten of swords is the irrevocable ending, being stabbed in the back, or an end of a cycle. The ending can be a relationship, a situation, or circumstance. Clearing the ground for something new. It can be the end of a delusion. A death of a concept or life direction. Lies or sadness.

The ten of pentacles are material abundance, family support, inheritance, money for property, selling or buying, and financial stability. It can indicate money coming from generations. Sharing talents or skills with the community. And alignment of one's will with spirit. Prosperity. Loosen up on possessions.

The wands are the fire signs of the zodiac: Aries, Leo, and Sagittarius.

The cups are the water signs of the zodiac: Cancer, Scorpio, and Pisces.

The swords are the air signs of the zodiac: Gemini, Libra, and Aquarius.

The pentacles are the earth signs of the zodiac: Taurus, Virgo, and Capricorn.

The Tarot Court Cards

PAGES

The Pages are the messengers in the tarot. The pages indicate forces in motion to stimulate change in growth.

The page of wands is a bearer of good news, growth, and knowledge, and is an enthusiastic messenger.

The page of cups can be news of a birth, new feelings or attitudes, a social message coming. It also could be new emotions and the beginning of a new friendship.

The page of swords requires quick thinking, decisiveness, and unexpected news, which can be upsetting or irritating. It indicates a complicated situation, gossip, or forceful communication.

The page of pentacles could be an opportunity to make money, although you may need to start at the bottom. It is a message of financial dealings. It could indicate education needed for financial gain.

KNIGHTS

The Knights are about movement and action.

The knights of wands can be an escape from difficulty, a change in the air. This card can indicate a long journey or a change of residence.

The knight of cups can be love or marriage coming into your life. Romance, artistic talent, or new relationships.

The knight of swords comes quickly but may die down in the chaos. It can be sudden changes or rapid comings and goings.

The knight of pentacles is a positive outcome of a situation, money coming to the client. Tangible progress, slow and steady.

QUEENS

The queens represent female energy and emotions.

The queen of wands is a professional, and she balances both family and career. This person may have several projects going on at one time.

The queen of cups can be a person who lives in a realm of fantasy and imagination. She can be a caring woman, with deep feelings, nurturing, and is highly psychic.

The queen of swords is a person of strong will and determination. She is intelligent and solitary, likes to be alone at times, and her head rules her heart.

The queen of pentacles is wise in business. She is a queen of fertility. She is a practical manager and uses a sensible approach in situations.

KINGS

The kings represent the male energy and authoritative figures.

The king of wands has a visionary look about him as well as boundless energy. He is a strong leader.

The king of cups is a caring, compassionate, sensitive person who may work in the helping professions. He is compassionate and is a wise counselor.

The king of swords makes his living through his intellect. He uses cool rationality and is authoritative and in command.

The king of pentacles is a practical person and a good businessman. He is concerned with finances.

Common Occupations for the Different People of the Tarot

The Wands people: these are the salespersons, the teachers, the preachers, the entrepreneurs.

The Cups people: These are the counselors, artists, musicians, psychics, welfare workers, and they are helping other people.

The Swords people: These are the intellectuals, journalists, travelers, doctors, lawyers, judges, and military leaders.

The Pentacles people: These are usually the bankers, businesspeople, accountants, laborers, farmers, and builders.

The Tarot and How I Give a Reading

Working with the tarot really helped me open up to my spiritual gifts and intuition. The tarot cards are never wrong, but sometimes, we may not interpret them correctly. Later, when the events take place, we will say, "Wow, now I know what the cards were talking about, and now I have a better understanding of what the cards were trying to tell me."

Because we live on the physical plane and work with the spiritual plane, timing can be different. I remember doing readings for people, and they would come back and say to me, "Yes, everything you said came true, but you were two months off." So, timing can be hard to predict. I usually try to give people a time, like around early spring, or within the next few months, this will happen.

When doing a reading, we are usually talking about the future, and time can change, and the outcome can change. Especially if the client chooses a different path or direction, then of course, it will change, and it will alter the outcome.

I remember doing a reading for a young Hispanic girl in her twenties, and I told her she was going to meet this guy and he was white, light-haired, and blue eyes, and she would fall madly in love with him, and they would eventually marry and have a life together. Well, she thought I was nuts! She said she would never be attracted to a white gringo man; it just would not happen. She told me that she was always attracted to the more Hispanic type of man with darker skin and dark features. Well, about three months later she came to see me and told me that yes, I was right, that she met a wonderful man, and he was light-haired and blue eyes and white skin. She could not believe how happy she was, and they were planning a life together. Of course, I was incredibly happy for her.

Sometimes, readings can seem very bizarre. I remember one of the first readings I gave to a woman, and I said," This is really strange, but I see you on a flying trapeze." She replied, "Well, that's not strange at all because I spent years in the circus." So, when doing a reading, it requires you to trust and have faith that you are delivering accurate, truthful messages because they are coming from the other side and being delivered with love.

When you are delivering the message to your client, you must have faith and trust that it is a message that is true. Even if that message does not make sense to you, it will make sense to the client. If not at that moment, it will in time. The whole purpose in doing readings is to give guidance, counseling, and help to the client looking for answers. You are trying to help your client on their spiritual path in life.

When I used to go to the psychic fairs in El Paso in the early eighties to late nineties, I would go five times a year, and it was remarkably busy. There would be lines leading out of the hotel from the lobby.

Every time I would go to the El Paso fair, I would exchange readings with my friend Houanne, who did palmistry readings. She was from England, and we were good friends. At the last fair that I saw Houanne, we decided to exchange readings as we usually did. It was very strange because when I held her hands, closed my eyes, and said the prayer to the other side, I heard distinctly from my guides, "This will be the last time you see her." I was surprised, but I did not say that to her, so I did the reading. However, as I did the reading, I felt like I was making the reading up. I did not seem to be receiving a lot of information to share with her. She asked about boyfriends and different things, and I was not getting a whole lot of answers. I just felt like I would do this reading for her even though, intuitively, I was not getting much. However, I did have the distinct impression that she had to be careful when driving or riding in the car, and I told her to put her angels around her when traveling in a vehicle. Two months later, I found out she had died in a car accident. Her boyfriend at the time was driving a motorhome in Houston, and they hit some slick water on the road and the vehicle flipped over and went off the road. She was riding in the back of the motorhome and died instantly.

Always trust your instincts and your intuition when doing a reading. It is never right to tell a client who you are reading that you see death; you could be wrong. You may advise them to be careful or that they may have a challenging time during a certain part of the year, but never tell them you see death. That is not your place to mention death because that is between their soul and God and is about divine intervention. It is also about their soul contract that they made before coming into this world. The experiences they chose to have here are for their spiritual growth. In doing a reading, do your best to give good advice in a loving way.

Giving a Reading

In a tarot reading, you use the cards and lay them out in a spread. There are many spreads, and I've included the one I designed in this book. One needs to find the one spread he or she is most comfortable using. The one I designed in the book is laid down, starting from left to right and then repeating using a second card over the first card you previously laid down.

When you feel blocked doing a card reading and not getting an intuitive thought or message on a card, go with the card's basic description and meaning.

First, you must set yourself up in an area where you and the client feel comfortable. Make sure this area feels sacred and blessed to you.

If, for some reason, you feel apprehensive about doing the reading for that person (for any reason), do not read for them. Only do a reading for someone professionally that is paying you in some way. This person can pay you in money or in a barter trade. If you decide to do readings professionally, you must be professional about it. In the beginning, it is okay to practice with family and friends while you are building up your confidence. In doing readings, you are tuning into your guides and your higher self, and this is not to be treated lightly or as a game. The reason you are reading for another is to help that person on a spiritual level.

Some clients will repeatedly come back with the same questions, and you give them the best advice you can, but sometimes they just want to hear what they want. It is up to each of us to make our best choices possible and live the best life that we can.

There are times when a client can become too dependent on the reader and schedule appointments too frequently. I do not feel this is healthy, and I usually advise people to come back for a reading in three months or more. Unless something unusual happens, they do not need reading that often. Even once a year will suffice. Usually, when I give a reading, it is good for at least six months, even though things are always changing. Six months is a good span of time for reading. If a client becomes too dependent on your readings and asks the same questions repeatedly, it may be time to turn them away because you cannot help them.

Clients can really drain your energy and sometimes you may feel like you are taking on their problems. Realize this is their spiritual path to learn and grow and not yours. Always send them away with blessings and love.

The Ritual

I prepare the room by smudging it with a white sage smudge stick, burning a Palo Santo stick, burning incense, lighting a candle, and spraying it with my blessing water.

I keep my cards stored in a special container, special cloth, special bag, or special box. I treat my cards with special love and care because they are sacred.

Lighting a candle draws away any negative energy and helps purify the area. I sometimes light incense unless the client opposes this.

In my reading room, I have statues, pictures of angels, saints, and other deities. I also have an ample collection of stones and crystals. I have my certifications on the walls. On the walls I also have suns and moons, and any artifacts that add beauty and light in the room. I also have crystal balls, a scrying mirror, pyramids, pendulums and a wealth of different tarot and oracle cards, as well as an assortment of other psychic tools.

When doing a reading, I shuffle my cards and put them together right-side up. I do not read reversals or my cards upside down. By shuffling the cards, I am putting my energy back into the cards. I usually make sure that I shuffle the cards at least seven times.

I then explain to the client what a tarot card reading is. I then ask the client to close their eyes and surround themselves with God's light (gold or white) while I say a brief prayer to the other side. I ask those on the other side that I can give this client truthful and helpful answers to any questions they may have. I also ask my guides, angels, and God to please protect the area that I am working in with love and light. And then I thank them because I cannot do this work by myself; I depend on those on the other side for help.

I then hand the cards to the client, and I ask that they shuffle the cards anyway they wish to, and if they wish to cut the deck they can do so; whatever makes them comfortable. When they are ready, I have them give the cards back to me. Now, the client is the one who has put their energy into the cards, and they will be the one choosing the cards for their reading. There is no mistake because they have chosen the cards, not you.

I now take the cards, lay them out in a spread, and proceed with the reading.

My Personal Tarot Spread

This is a spread that I created and use frequently. You can design whatever spread works for you, or you can use a spread that other people have created.

I close my eyes, connect with the other side, and ask in a prayer that I receive honest, accurate and truthful answers in my reading.

I proceed to lay down one card at a time, a total of seven cards, starting on the left-hand side and working to the right-hand side. Then, once again, I will lay out seven more cards in the same manner as the previous cards.

If I need a better understanding of the messages of the cards I have laid down, I will lay out six more cards on the side. These six cards will give me more confirmation on the reading.

The seven positions of the tarot cards:

- The position of the first two cards speaks of the past and what has been going on.

- The position of the second two cards speaks of the present and what is happening now.

- The position of the third two cards speaks of the future and what to expect.

- The position of the fourth two cards speaks of what procedure to take.

- The position of the fifth two cards speaks of negative or positive energies.

- The position of the sixth two cards speaks of hopes and fears.

- The position of the seventh two cards speaks of the future outcome.

- Then, the remaining six cards will help explain the reading even further.

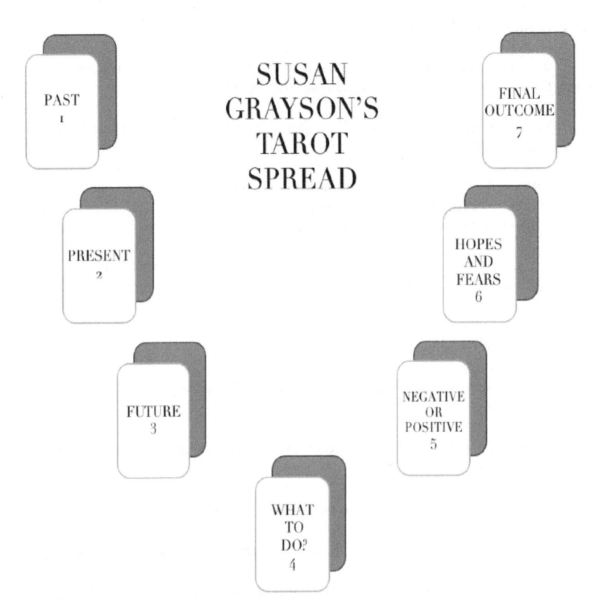

Chapter Four: My Move to Corpus Christi, Texas

Before deciding to move from Albuquerque, I got my minister's license and hypnotherapy certification. I enjoyed being an officiant at weddings and other celebrations, as well as doing past life regressions with my clients.

In 1996, I decided I wanted to move back to the ocean. Being originally from Boston, I missed the water and salt air. I was ready to make a move, but I knew I did not want to move to a cold coastal area.

One day, I got a map of the country, and after saying a prayer to the other side and asking for divine help, I picked out six different areas that were along the coast in which to move. Starting from the east coast in South Carolina down to Florida, I worked my way down to the gulf and up the west coast to California. I narrowed the choices down to six locations and I would choose from these places.

I brought out my pendulum and tarot cards, and with the help of my guides, angels, God, and helpers from the other side, I proceeded to find the perfect place for me.

I knew there was a Psychic Fair coming up in Corpus Christi, Texas, and that may be a place I should consider moving to. Therefore, I signed up for the psychic fair in Corpus Christi and planned to go there and check it out.

I listed Corpus Christi as one of my options. I said a few prayers and asked the pendulum to pick a place that I would be happy and successful living in. I also laid out my tarot cards with the same question in mind. After carefully using the pendulum on the map as well as tarot cards, I received my divine answer. The perfect place was shown to me to be Corpus Christi. This was shown to me to be the perfect place for my success and happiness.

I then put in my application to do the Psychic Fair in Corpus Christi and made plans to attend it as a reader. So, I went to the Corpus Christi fair and the rest is history. I just knew in my heart and soul I had to move there, and I moved to Corpus Christi in 1996 and fell in love with it.

While at the fair in Corpus Christi, I did a reading for a woman named Jana, who owned a New Age bookstore called Angel Light. After the reading I did for her, she told me that if I decided to move there, she would offer me a job at her store doing readings. She did this because she was impressed by her own reading that I had given her.

So, it was set in motion; I moved to Corpus and started working at Angel Light for Jana. I worked at Angel Light, worked as a teacher's aide at the public schools in Corpus Christi, and did readings in my apartment.

Working for Jana at Angel Light was a wonderful experience and I learned how much work having a store could be. I wanted to have this knowledge of all the workings that go on in the store and how to manage situations. I learned a great deal while I was working there. It was a beautiful store and had a heavenly atmosphere surrounding it.

Before I moved to Corpus, and while at the psychic fair there, I met a wonderful man for whom I did a reading. Finally, I met a man who was on the same spiritual path as I was, and he was a person that I could continue to grow with. His name was Bill, and we were together for five years. We got married and have been together for over 21 years. I cannot praise my husband enough because he has supported me in every way possible, emotionally, physically, and spiritually.

With the help of my husband, Bill, and my son, Juan, we opened a metaphysical store in Corpus Christi in 1998. We called it The Dreamworker. This was a dream come true. I met such wonderful people there, and they remain friends even today.

The store did well for eight years, and then I decided to sell it and move back to Albuquerque to help my daughter with her three girls. I had been away for 10 years in Corpus Christi, and although I loved it and found it to be a wonderful place to live, I knew it was time to leave. I felt after ten years, I needed to get to know my granddaughters.

I have great memories of the ten years I lived in Corpus. Especially during the eight years that I had the store, because I thoroughly enjoyed it. While having the store, I would do readings on the radio station every Monday for a year and a half. I also did some events on a television station. Being on the radio and the television station was a wonderful opportunity to promote my store and business.

In my store, we sold books, tarot cards, jewelry, consignment items, crystals and stones, statues, new age music, and so many more items related to the metaphysical. At the store, we also held belly dancing, yoga, meditation, and psychometry classes one night a week.

I will always be thankful to Jana and working at Angel Light for the experiences it gave me. I will always be indebted to my dear friends Mitch and Wes in Albuquerque. I did readings at their store prior to moving to Corpus. Mitch and Wes gave me all the information that I needed to start The Dreamworker. They helped me by giving me all the information as to what merchandise to order and from where. They had their store since 1980, called Blue Eagle Metaphysical Emporium in Albuquerque. Their store is still going strong today! They were so generous in helping me with all their knowledge, information, and expertise. The information they gave me was the start I needed, and I will always be grateful to them. Being in Corpus Christi was a wonderful experience, and I would not trade it for the world.

While in Corpus, I taught psychic development classes and did past life regressions with clients. I was also an officiant at weddings, funerals, and christenings.

Bill and I were ministers at The Chapel of Spiritual Light in Corpus, a nondenominational church. Being ministers at the chapel was a beautiful experience for the two of us. Bill and I had such a wonderful congregation of people there, and we will always cherish the memories we had at the chapel.

After moving back to Albuquerque in 2006, I continued to work part-time, giving readings at Blue Eagle. I still attended the psychic fairs and continued teaching classes at that store.

In 2018, I felt as though I had grown stagnant in my psychic work, and I needed a place where I could expand my knowledge and continue to grow.

Then, in 2018, my son was offered a job in Phoenix, Arizona. This was a message from above to make another move and the answer to my prayers. So, we followed my son to Phoenix.

Bill and I found a spiritualist church that we fell in love with called Rising Phoenix. We took some mediumship classes there, and they were wonderful. I realized that through my readings, I had been doing mediumship all along. We continued studying the mediumship classes and loved it.

In 2019, Bill and I went to Arthur Findlay College in Stanstead, England and studied mediumship with the tutors there. What an awesome experience it was for us learning and practicing mediumship!

Then, in 2021, I went to Lily Dale in New York with a dear friend, Tina (a friend and mediumship teacher). We studied Forensic Mediumship with Thomas John (a world-renowned medium) for a week at the spiritualist camp.

When we first moved to Phoenix, Bill and I took classes Monday nights with Tina on Mediumship. She is just an awesome, kind, and generous person who gives so much of herself to teaching others. Her classes are great and are a mixture of professional mediums and psychics as well as novices.

I have taught mediumship and intuitive development classes at Rising Phoenix Spiritualist Church.

Bill and I have a healing group at our home, and we meet once a month and continue learning from each other.

I also participate on Tuesday evenings in a psychic squad on Zoom. This is run by our dear friend Don Rumer-Rivera, whom I met in Tina's class. Every week, Don gives us exercises on Zoom, which enhances our abilities. Don has been instrumental in helping me do free readings live on Facebook and YouTube once a week. He has mastered his abilities in the technical world of computers. He is a great medium and friend to Bill and me. Don is responsible for helping me design my logo, which I love.

I am thankful to all the people who have helped me along the way. Obviously, my loved ones, guides, and angels were instrumental in picking these people.

Chapter Five: Pendulum Magick History

Pendulums have been used as a tool for divination and dowsing for thousands of years. Their use has been recorded as far back as 8,000 years ago. The pendulum is a great tool because it makes us stop, breathe, relax, and go within.

Early hypnotists used the pendulum to relax their patients into a deep state of meditation. It enabled the patients to go into that relaxed state as they repeatedly watched the pendulum move back and forth.

Dowsing with a pendulum can give us guidance and answers to help us locate resources. The pendulum can be used to locate underground resources such as water, oil, metals, and crystals.

You can use the pendulum for divination purposes, such as answering basic yes or no questions. You may also contact your guides, angels, or ancestors with this tool.

Pendulums can be used in energy healing work, such as balancing the chakras and locating infections, ailments, and allergies in your body. They can also be used to clear spaces and find lost items. The pendulum can help you determine a baby's gender. To receive the best results, working with the pendulum requires a lot of practice.

Pendulums are usually cone-shaped and made of metal, wood, crystals, or stones and hang from a chain. It must have some weight at the end of the chain and be heavy enough to create a swinging motion.

How Does a Pendulum Work?

The pendulum works by responding to your own body's energetic field in conjunction with your higher self and your intuition. It creates a jerk reflex in your arm and wrist that allows the pendulum to move in a certain direction to answer your question. The movement in your wrists and arms are moved by your subconscious activity in your brain and called the "ideomotor reflex."

When you use the pendulum, your energy field responds subconsciously to what your inner self already knows. The pendulum swings because of the electromagnetic field on Earth. It is a transmitter of energy and moves accordingly. The answers you receive are always the answers within you.

Chakra Balancing

You can check the balance of someone's chakras by placing the pendulum one to two inches above their body. If their chakras are balanced, the pendulum will move in a circular clockwise motion. If the person's chakras are unbalanced, the pendulum will move in an irregular sideways pattern or will not move at all.

How to Remedy the Situation

If the chakras are unbalanced, spin the pendulum over the chakra area three times in a clockwise motion, then counter-clockwise three times, then again clockwise three times. This will shift and disturb the stagnant energy so that the chakra can spin freely again, allowing balance and ease back into that person's life.

Then, place the pendulum above the chakra again and watch if it is spinning freely in a clockwise circular motion. If not, repeat the process until it is. Then, place the appropriate crystal or stone over the area to boost the healing process. You may also use the pendulum when doing Reiki, oneness blessing, or other healing modalities.

Programming Your Pendulum

Before using the pendulum, say a silent prayer or an affirmation. You might say, "My spirit is guiding and directing my pendulum use in dowsing." Or you can say, "My mind is open and receptive to the answers I get from my spirit through the pendulum." Another statement may be, "My pendulum will give me honest and truthful answers to my questions." Any of these positive statements can work for you.

When Working with the Pendulum

1. Find a comfortable and quiet place to sit and relax. Close your eyes for a minute and focus within. Focus on your breathing. Breathe in slowly to the count of five, holding your breath for the count of four, and breathing out for the count of four. Do this a few times to totally relax you.

2. Hold the chain (connecting the stone or metal) between your thumb and forefinger. The chain should hang down 4 to 5 inches with the stone or metal connected to the bottom of the chain.

3. Let the pendulum hang perfectly still.

4. Ask the pendulum to move, and give you a yes answer. Mentally ask the pendulum to move forward and backward or in a side-to-side movement. This is your "yes" answer. While doing this, keep your fingers, hands, and wrists still. Then, mentally, tell the pendulum to stop moving.

5. Then, ask your pendulum to show you your "no" answer, which will be the opposite of the yes movement.

6. Then, tell your pendulum to stop.

7. Practice asking yes and no questions. You can also practice with various charts. You can make your own full pie-shaped or half pie-shaped chart, writing on the sections whatever you want to know.

8. Then, hold your pendulum from the point from which all the sections lead and allow it to give you the answer to your questions.

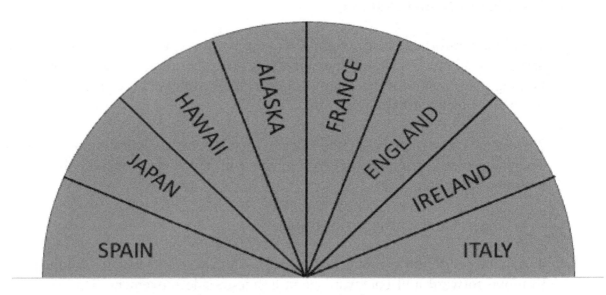

Where should I go on vacation?
EXAMPLE OF A HALF PIE-SHAPED
PENDULUM CHART

Clearing Spaces

You can clear negative, stagnant, and unwanted energy from spaces and people. To do so, follow the procedure below:

1. Sit comfortably in an area of your home where you can have a private space with no interruptions. Now, state your wish to clear the energy in the room and remove any negative energy that has existed there. Ask that only good, positive energy exists in this space. Now, hold the pendulum out in front of you.

2. Say your prayer, then ask the pendulum to move any stagnant, negative, or unwanted energy from this place to be buried deep within Mother Earth.

3. The negative energy will change in Mother Earth and turn into positive energy.

4. It does not matter which direction the pendulum moves because it still clears the negative energy from the place.

5. While doing this and allowing the pendulum to swing the way it needs to, visualize the process of white light coming from above and surrounding you while you are clearing all negative energy and sending it down into Mother Earth.

6. Once the energy has cleared, the pendulum will start slowing down and moving in a different direction. By the pendulum moving in a different direction, you will know the area has been cleared, and the positive, beautiful energy has been restored.

Other Uses for the Pendulum

You may design your own chart, either a full pie or a half pie chart, and by filling in the appropriate words, you can find many answers to the questions you seek. Some examples of using the pendulum are:

- You can scan your pet's body for energy and health issues.

- You can assess the freshness of food.

- Test for allergy and food intolerances.

- To see if your water is safe to drink.

- To do map dowsing.

- To locate missing people, animals, or objects.

- To see what vitamins and minerals your body may need.

- Where you should take your next vacation.

- Where should you move to for happiness, success, relationships, and good health?

How to Choose a Pendulum

Just like choosing tarot cards, just because they are beautiful does not mean that a pendulum will work for you. You need to connect with its energy and feel a strong vibe that resonates with you. When you hold it, feel that energy and see if it feels like the right pendulum for you. It should go with the flow of your thoughts, and your energy should connect comfortably with it.

The more love you give your pendulum, the more it will give back to and work for you. Make sure you place it in a special bag, cloth, or box and keep it in a sacred area.

Intention is the key to cleansing and working with your pendulum. Your thoughts create your reality. First, you must clear the energy on the pendulum from the factory from which it came. Ask in a calm and meditative state for the old and stagnant energy to be removed and transferred to the ground to Mother Earth.

You can use herbs to cleanse your pendulum, including a white sage smudge stick, Palo Santo, rosemary, mugwort, lavender, eucalyptus leaves, cedar, or sweet grass. Burning any of these and running the smoke around your pendulum will cleanse it.

If the smoke is thick and gray, it means a lot of negative energy was on your pendulum, but if the smoke was light, then it was not so much.

Use a dish or abalone shell underneath to catch the embers.

If you wish, you can place your pendulum in a beautiful garden or potted plant. Do this at the beginning of a full moon and leave it in the soil for an entire moon cycle. However, try not to bury the stainless-steel chain, as it may rust.

After cleansing your pendulum, run fresh water over it.

You can also place your pendulum on the windowsill at the full moon and leave it there all night. You can retrieve it the next day at dawn. It will absorb the beautiful moonlight and energy from the moon.

Except for amethyst, citrine, rose quartz, fluorite, and smoky quartz, you can place your pendulum in the sunlight. The above-mentioned stones will fade in the sunlight.

You can also place your pendulum in spring water or filtered water. You may also use Reiki symbols or oneness blessing symbols to cleanse it before using it. Or you may visualize white light in the water giving the pendulum pure, positive, blessed energy.

You can also bury your pendulum in a bowl of sea salt, Himalayan rock salt, or sand from the beach, which will purify it.

Another suggestion would be to place your crystal pendulums in a storage bag with black obsidian, selenite, or black tourmaline stones, which will protect your crystals from negative energy.

Dowsing, Water Witching, Doodle Bugging or Questing

Dowsing is a method that has been used for thousands of years. There are some 8,000-year-old wall paintings in African caves that depict a man with a forked stick dowsing for water.

There are also some 4,000-year-old Chinese and Egyptian artworks showing dowsing. Moses was known to use dowsing rods to locate water.

During Europe's Middle Ages and in 17th century France, dowsing was used to locate coal deposits as well as escaped criminals.

There are an estimated 30,000 dowsers known in the United States. The American Society of Dowsers was founded in 1961.

Every major water pipeline company in the US has a dowser on their payroll.

When I was at Arthur Findlay College in England, we were shown how vibrations in our bodies were raised and lowered using dowsing rods.

In many industries, dowsing has been effective in locating buried cables, water, gas lines, minefields, all coins, jewelry, weapons tossed in the lake, and murdered victims. The pendulum is usually used on a map first to identify these suggestive locations.

Dowsing is to search with a rod or pendulum for anything.

Dowsing is the ability to tune in to some force that science has not yet identified. It is a way to contact your intuitive side.

First, you must send an intent or request to the instrument to target or locate a specific object.

In dowsing, water flowing underground causes an electric current. Anytime electricity flows in any kind of conductor, it creates a magnetic field. Using a dowsing instrument allows your subconscious mind to tap into the wealth of information available from the subconscious mind.

We can tune into electrical currents and contact energy that we are not conscious of. Relax, have faith, and learn to trust the instruments.

L-RODS

L-Rods are the most popular because they are easy to make and use. They are L-shaped and made from metal or copper.

1. Point the dowsing rods straight forward for the "ready" position.

2. The L rods will cross over each other for "yes" when over the target.

3. The L rods will swing outward for the "no "response.

Y-RODS

Y-Rods are forked sticks or talking sticks. Usually about 12 to 24 inches long and an 8th to 1/4 inch in diameter. They are usually made from a tree branch.

Hold each branch of the Y, palms facing up with the end pointing down.

1. The ready position is pointing upward at 45°.

2. When the Y-rod swings down from the "ready "position, it will mean "yes."

3. When the Y-rod swings upward from the "ready "position, it means "no."

Since the Y-rod only uses up-and-down motion, you will need to turn your body to find the correct direction.

You are not teaching the pendulum or the dowsing rods to do certain things; you are the dowsing system.

The wording of the question you ask is the most important part of dowsing. The Dowser needs to be specific in directing the question. For instance, you should ask the L-rod to point to the Earth's magnetic west. The dowsing system takes words and phrases literally. Do not use ambiguous phrases; be specific on what you want to know. And practice, practice, and practice.

Chapter Six: Psychic Protection

There are times in our lives when we need psychic protection, and it can be for several reasons.

We may need protection from individuals who have ill thoughts or intentions against us, and these can be ordinary people like your neighbors, coworkers, friends, or family members.

Or you need protection from places or locations where they can retain the vibrations of a disturbing situation or vibrations of past residents. It may be an area where souls on the other side have left their imprints in a place where they experienced a tragic passing.

You may need protection from items or things that hold onto the negative vibrations of a previous owner or a previous predicament. An example could be a home, vehicle, land, establishment, business, etc.

All these situations would warrant some psychic protection.

Jesus, Buddha, Mary, and many other loving ascended masters have been depicted with a crown of light around their heads. The light comes from the Greek word aura, which means breath or air. The light around their heads and bodies comes from within them. It shows that they possess a perfect balance of body, mind, and soul.

Have you ever felt physically, mentally, or spiritually drained just talking to someone?

We call these people energy vampires because they drain our energy and leave us exhausted. They can unknowingly or intentionally do this.

If these people have malicious intent, it could result in an injury from them out of revenge or vindication. Victims can become attacked by the use of force from the thoughts of that malicious individual. Those people may harbor hatred or bitterness for another human being, wishing them ill or bad luck.

These unwelcome energy vampires will endlessly dump us with their severe problems or tales of woe. They will have a "poor me" approach to life and want everyone to fix things for them. An example of these people could be one in authority over another person, such as a boss, parent, friend, or relative. These people bring stress to another person. This also includes people with tempers or anger issues.

Some unknown examples would be door-to-door salespeople who are very persistent, people who talk endlessly about themselves and are not interested in anything you have to say.

You can also be under attack in a dysfunctional relationship. These are absorbing, conflicting individuals, such as partners who do not pull their own weight, and they can be sucking you dry.

A good example of people susceptible to psychic attacks may be in the healthcare business, such as those working in the emergency room. They are susceptible because they are experiencing the sight of blood, the screams of pain, and the smells of chemicals, and they must touch the patient. Some spirits of the people who have died in the hospital have followed home their nurses, not aware they have passed over. Other professions susceptible to psychic attacks are:

- Dentist, because of the pain inflicted on their patients.

- Airline professionals because of the people who have a fear of flying.

- Law enforcement because they deal with life and death situations.

- Legal professionals, because of the stress the client's experience.

- Salespeople, because of the stress involved.

- Sometimes, working all day with computers can cause one to absorb radiation.

- Living near high-tension power lines is unhealthy.

- Some of these cures can be used to ward against psychic attacks:

- Airline professionals can carry stones such as petrified wood or tiger's eye.

- The law-enforcement person can carry a bloodstone on them for courage or wear a St. Christopher medal.

- People in the creative arts and agents can keep a small plant on their desk.

Psychic Protection

If you cannot avoid working with computers all day or living by high-tension power lines, use magnetic therapy. Another remedy is to carry a malachite stone on your person or place it near the computer or electronic devices.

You can absorb a lot of negative energy in bar rooms, so please protect yourself. Sometimes, individuals who have passed over have a lot of addictions, and hanging around the bars and attaching their energy to a live person feeds their addictions.

A hex would be considered a black magick voodoo doll.

A curse means to conjure up. One would place this curse upon a person or a group of people with the intention of causing them harm.

An example of this would be King Tut's tomb in Egypt. Over his tomb at the entrance, it says "Death will slay with his wings whoever disturbs the peace of this Pharaoh," hence this is the mummy's curse.

Ghosts

A poltergeist is a very noisy spirit. Whereas an apparition makes no noise; it appears and then vanishes.

A Specter is a haunting or disturbing image that comes back repeatedly.

An example of ghosts is in the Himalayas, where the people who fear burial rituals will write the deceased's name on bamboo paper and then burn it.

In the West Indies, widows wear red underwear to ward off dead husbands.
The reason people wore black when in mourning was to be made invisible to the dead.

As far as spells go, do not pay for a spell to be removed. Do it yourself. When you wish to remove someone and banish them from your life, do it for 2 to 3 days when the moon is dark.

Please make sure there are no interruptions and no phones, and that you do it in total privacy. A spell is more effective if you do it yourself.

Never put negative spells on someone because you cannot escape the consequences of one's actions. Spells are used to fulfill something you want in your life. You must have the proper intention and honestly believe you can achieve the desired results. Remember, what goes around comes around. Always work in love and light.

Protective stones that you can carry on you and can use for protection are:

- Quartz crystals: you can program them for any purpose.

- Chrysolite: which helps with emotional balance.

- Fluorite: a calming stone.

- Jet: this stone reduces stress and relieves depression.

- Lapis Lazuli: boosts the immune system.

- Pink Coral: It is soothing and resolves conflicts.

- Amethyst: dispels anxiety and aids one in focus.

- Chalcedony: gets rid of nightmares.

- Red Coral: Shields one from harm.

- Obsidian: Removes all negativity.

- Moldavite: for protection.

- Black Tourmaline: banishes evil and negative energy.

- Malachite: protects against radiation.

To charge water with crystals, put them under the moonlight on the windowsill. The following day, after they are charged, pass your hands over the glass of water, then remove the crystals and drink the water.

Charms and Amulets used for Protection:

- Crosses: Wear them, hang them in the house, or put them on shields.

- Pentagrams: The five points represent the earth, air, fire, water, and spirit.

- Bells: Ring them to dispel evil forces.

- Circles: Because they are a continuous line, they represent no beginning, no end, and life everlasting.

- Saint Christopher medals and aquamarine stones: Carry these on you when traveling.

- Peacock feather: Place in the home for serenity and harmony.

- Dragons and Gargoyles: Statues used to ward off evil and give protection over their communities.

- Tigers or Lions: Place on door knockers; the demons fear the tigers or lions.

- Eye of Horus: The symbol Egyptians used for protection, health, and restoration.

- Evil eye from Turkey: Hang above baby's crib or in the house for protection. Wards off variations of evil intentions.

- Anchor: For security, safety, and stability.

- Angel statues and pictures: For divine protection.

- Rose of Jericho: Place the plant in a bowl with one inch of water. As the plant opens and expands, sprinkle the water with your hands throughout the house to bless and protect it.

Protection by Use of the Runes

The word Runes means a secret or mystery. It is a 24-letter alphabetic script created among the Germanic tribes at least two thousand years ago. It is linked to religious beliefs and practices. Although it has never been a spoken language, the Runes were a system whose sacred function was to permit communication between humankind and the gods.

By the fourth century A.D., the runes were becoming widely known in northern Europe. The original Germanic or Elder Futhark is composed of twenty-four letters and existed as early as the second century B.C. By the ninth century A.D., the alphabetic variation known as the Younger Futhark was reduced to sixteen letters, while later Anglo-Saxon Futhark alphabets expanded to include as many as thirty-three letters.

From the ninth through the twelfth century, the Norseman carried the runes to Anglo-Saxon England, then to Iceland, and then to wherever the long voyages took them. Influenced by the tribal wisdom of northern Europe, the Viking runes emerged.

Runes were used to influence the weather, the tides, crops, matters of love and healing; there were runes of fertility, cursing and removing curses, birth, and death. Runic glyphs were carved into bone, cut into leather, and pieces of wood.

The Runes were carved on swords, amulets, rings, and bracelets and painted on homes for protection. There are still Runes seen on memorials to Viking warriors on huge standing stones along the roads and fields throughout Scandinavia.

In early times, runes were related to magick. A Rune Master would use these symbols because they represented his command of supernatural powers.

The Rune used for protection is an ALGIZ. This Rune serves as a mirror for the spiritual warrior. The warrior's protection is like the curved horns of the elk, or the rustle of sedge grass; for both serve to keep open the space around you. This Rune has been known to protect you against enemies and against evil. It symbolizes the elk with its powerful antlers that can protect one from the enemy. This Rune also stands for awareness and connects man with God.

Protecting Yourself and Your Home

Prayers are an issue of faith and trust. Saying prayers daily or doing meditations helps you connect with the other side. Your angels and your spiritual guides are your strongest allies and are always with you. They love you and want the best for you. Always surround yourself with the white light covering your entire body. Make sure you surround yourself with the angelic white light when traveling in a vehicle, in your home, or wherever you may be. While away from your home, it would be a clever idea to always keep your aura close to your body, especially when in crowds or in uneasy or unfamiliar situations or environments. When leaving your home, visualize that golden white light surrounding your home and your pets, and ask the angels to take care of everything while you are away.

One time, when I was living in Albuquerque, I left the apartment to teach a class. Before I left the apartment, I stopped for a minute. I thought, "Oh no, I haven't protected my place in a long time." I stopped and visualized that golden white light surrounding my apartment and asked the angels for their protection in guarding my apartment. Upon arriving home after teaching my class, I noticed the fire trucks surrounding the apartment complex. Both apartments adjacent to mine were on fire, but thankfully, my apartment was not affected at all. I know it was because I enlisted the help of my angels to protect my place.

The angels are always with you, but you need to ask them for protection.

Do not be afraid to ask for yourself as well as for others. Send your prayers up to the angels and ask them for help, and if needed, ask for help for your loved ones. Ask the angels to protect them, guide them, and surround them with love. Angels can perform miracles because they are not in the physical world but in the spiritual world. All our prayers are heard, and sometimes they are granted immediately, but sometimes they are not.

House Cleansings

To do a house cleansing, you will need the following:

- A smudge stick, which can be made from either sage, cedar, or sweetgrass. This will be used in a sweeping motion with your hand to spread the smoke around. You may wish to place a small plate or an abalone shell under the lit smudge stick to keep the burnt embers from catching fire on your carpet; you can also use the feather to sweep the smoke around.

- Blessing water, which I make my own. Or you can use holy water.

- You will need sea salt.

- Several tea light candles,

- A lighter, a feather, a coffee can, an abalone shell, and a pendulum if you wish.

Starting from inside of the house, open the front window a couple of inches. Then, standing on the inside of the house behind the front door, say a prayer to your angels, guides, God, or any divine deity you wish to call in. Ask these divine helpers to remove all negative energy from this home. Any unwanted spirits that are present in the home must also leave. Then, ask these divine helpers to replace all negative energy with pure, positive energy and to bless this home with their love.

If there are unwanted spirits in the home, ask those divine helpers to send them to the light where their loved ones are waiting for them.

I then proceed with the ritual:

Take the tea light candles and place one in each room in a safe area. Then, lighting the candle, say your prayer. You will move from room to room, starting at the front door in a clockwise manner. Light the candles while saying a prayer to bring loving energy and protection into this home and to remove all negative energy. Visualize all negative energy leaving the home through the front open window.

Make sure while cleansing the home, you are also cleansing the garage, patio, tool shed, or attached buildings as part of the house.

Next, while still in a clockwise direction in each room, sprinkle a pinch of sea salt in every corner, including the closets. As you place sea salt in every corner of the rooms and garage, say your prayer to remove all negative energy. Leave the sea salt in every corner for 24 hours before removing it.

Now, you will go to each room again, and in the same direction (clockwise), spray your holy water or blessing water in every corner of every room and garage. Do not forget to say your prayers while you are doing this.

Now, for the last step, you will light your smudge stick standing at the back of the front door in the house, and with prayers, smudge yourself well. Then, proceed to smudge every room in the clockwise direction. You must make sure that the smoke goes into every area, whether it be the drawers, the closets, the cabinets, the refrigerator, the microwave, the oven, or the dishwasher. The smoke must penetrate every room and in every place, as well as the garage.

Every area must be smudged completely while saying your prayer.

After smudging the entire home and garage, you may use your pendulum to see if everything feels clear. If an area appears questionable, say some more prayers in that space. Now, you can either place the smudge stick in an empty coffee can to let it burn out naturally, or douse it with water.

Now, going back to the front door, thank your angels, guides, God, and any other deity that helped you cleanse your home. Your place should now feel light and blessed.

Daily Protection

The white or gold light is a symbol of spirituality that is used in meditation. It is the God light, and the angelic light that always protects us.

Every day, being out in the world, we are surrounded by negative energy. It is a promising idea to do a daily cleansing on yourself. Being around large groups of people and uncomfortable environments can bring energy to you that can become uncomfortable and chaotic.

An effective way to cleanse yourself is to visualize a cascade of water flowing over you and going down the drain or to take a shower, removing any negative energy that has attached to your aura and then seeing it go down the drain.

Laughter will create lightness and will ward off negative attacks.

Other items used for protection:

Hang a dreamcatcher in your bedroom near your bed to catch the bad dreams.

Make a dream pillow to help you sleep and protect you against nightmares. You can use any of the herbs below on your pillow.

Effective herbs used for protection are Bay laurel, blackberry, cedar, cinnamon, frankincense, mugwort, muller, sandalwood, St. John's wort, and thyme.

Essential oils used for protection are lavender, Jasmine, hyacinth, bergamot, marjoram, and valerian.

Chapter Seven: Psychometry

In July 2021, I was in Lily Dale, New York, studying Forensic Mediumship with Thomas John for a week. The class was remarkably interesting, and one day, we had the opportunity to hold a plastic baggie with an item in it that was on that person when they died. The item that I got to hold was a tissue inside the baggie. The tissue was in the victim's pocket of her dress when she passed. As soon as I held the baggie with the tissue in it, I could feel and see how the woman passed. She had been on top of a stairwell in her home the second floor, and a young woman came behind her and pushed her. As a result, she fell down the stairs and died. The vision was so real to me, and because I had the opportunity to hold the object, I was able to witness the last moments of the woman's life.

Psychometry is the ability to hold an object and get a sensation from that object.

It is the ability to describe the feeling associated with that object in pictures. You can sense characteristic qualities or energies emanating from that object in past, present, or future events associated with the person who handled, used, or wore that object.

Psychometry is the process of transferring psychic vibrations from your hands (while touching the object) to your solar plexus. The solar plexus is the third chakra above your navel and is extremely sensitive. It is the main feeling and psychic reception area in your body. When you hold the object in your hand, note the impressions you receive in your solar plexus.

Pay attention to where your intuition comes from. Do you get visual images?

Symbolisms? Sounds? Do you hear voices? Do you feel a body sensation, like being touched? Do you feel heat or cold?

As you practice doing psychometry and become more aware of your senses, it will help make your psychic abilities stronger.

Get into the habit of listening by closing your eyes and paying attention to the sounds around you. Name them, count them, and imitate them. Listen to the changes in the wind and the sounds of the leaves in the trees, the birds singing, the cars driving by, the laughter of children playing, the dogs barking, everything in your environment that surrounds you.

Learn to focus on smells, the aromas that instantly trigger your systems, especially the part associated with memory and emotions. These smells include those of the past, such as perfumes worn by a loved one, cookies baked by your grandmother, cigarette or cigar smoke, and different smells associated with people who have passed. This will help you connect with them and their energy.

When you are eating, go slowly and really taste the flavors in your food.

Notice how different objects have different feelings, such as rough, smooth, soft, or hard.

Practice sensory exercises indoors and outdoors.

By practicing, you will sharpen your awareness and have fun.

Sit and study people at a mall or bus stop. Try to guess what they are thinking: Are they nice, angry, loving, serious, compassionate, or self-absorbed? Notice their facial appearance and expressions and the way they carry themselves. Pay attention to the energy that surrounds them. How do you feel when you observe them? What unique or distinguishable characteristics do you sense about them?

When you must decide, is it your priority to feel comfortable with the solution, do you visualize all the possibilities, or do you pick the most logical answer?

When you buy new clothes, jewelry, a car, or furniture, do you choose these things that you feel comfortable with? Or is it a trendier item?

Get to know yourself and how you are most sensitive. Also, get in the habit of paying attention to what is happening around you. Instead of moving automatically from moment to moment, hour to hour, and place to place like a zombie, zero in on an object and focus on it. Be aware of every moment.

When you zero in on an object and focus on it, look at every part of it, including its color, shape, and everything about it. Everything you feel, see, hear, taste, and smell, ask yourself how it affects you and how it makes you feel. Does it bring up any emotions, good or bad? Does the object make you feel good? Remind you of old happy times? Or do you feel sad?

Keep sensing that object until you are satisfied that you have felt all the vibrational impressions of that object. Run your hands over the object and note the feelings produced in your solar plexus as you touch or pass over the item with your hands.

Be aware of all your feelings. For example, how do you sense a room when you first enter physically? How does it feel when you first meet a person and shake their hands?

A person with a high clairvoyant sense would see all the colors, objects, and shapes.

A clairaudience individual would hear thoughts or words of conversations that took place there. Anyone with high intuition would just know what happened in the room.

Those high in clairsentience will sense the vibrations in the room with their feelings.

How do you form impressions when you meet people for the first time? Developing your psychic abilities is all about being aware of your feelings, not your practical ideas or programmed thoughts on things; it is all about feelings.

# Chapter Eight: Candle Magick

Candles are used in most ceremonies and rituals. An example of this would be in an environment such as churches. Candles are burned and used because they cause an altered state of awareness and produce changes in the environment and circumstances. For example, dinner by candlelight creates a very relaxing, romantic, and peaceful mood, or birthday wishes that come true after blowing out all the candles on the cake.

When using candles for a spell or ritual, always let the candle burn out or use the snuffer when extinguishing a flame; do not blow out the candle.

When casting spells during the new or waning moon, life energy decreases. So, you would use this time to banish or decrease. An example of this would be casting spells to get rid of something such as an illness, issues with a troublesome neighbor, harassment, or a lawsuit. Use the full to dark moon for these situations.

You would do spellcasting during the full moon or the waxing moon when life energy is increasing. This is the time to activate, vitalize, and increase things. A time to gain or build up some things such as love, money, etc... It is also the time to create something new. You would begin this ritual at the new moon to the full moon.

Crescent Moon

This is the time of the moon when there is the first sliver of light. Do your ritual at this time to mark new beginnings, endeavors, and relationships.

Waxing Moon to New Moon - First Quarter

This lasts for three days of the first quarter. This is the time for a ritual that would be good for fertility magick, the beginning of a love affair, to increase health and well-being. This is a time to plant magickal herbs. This is also a time to draw things to you and finalize plans, expansion, development, and growth. This is a time to increase things of your own, your knowledge, bank accounts, and relationships. Lunar and solar forces work together, pulling things in the same direction.

Full Moon - Second Quarter

This is the high tide of magick psychic powers. The sun and moon are opposite, which allows the sun's full light to shine on the moon. It is a time of illumination, completion, unrest, and using what we worked to create. The most potent time is three days prior to the full moon and the actual time of the full moon. This is the time to increase your psychic ability. It is the time of fulfillment, activity, perfecting ideas, becoming organized, celebrating, and renewing commitments to people or projects. And the best time for spells of any kind.

Waning Moon - From Full To Black-Third Quarter

This is the time for undoing, receding, eliminating, and separating. Peaceful endings to a love affair or a business partnership. Letting go of past experiences or letting go of an undesired part of yourself. This is a time to lose weight, cut herbs and flowers, and complete projects. A time to cast away, let go and release, break unhealthy habits, resolve issues, and deal with legal matters at this time.

Black Moon - No Moon-Fourth Quarter

This is resting time. It is best not to attempt any magick at all. It is time to draw back, reorganize and reflect on what has passed. Time to rid yourself of what has become unnecessary to make room for what is new that is coming in. Time for disintegration. Time for gaining understanding, contemplation, meditation, and preparation. Time for seeking spiritual guidance. This is a good time for seclusion.

Blue Moon - Magickal Moon

This is when two moons occur in the same calendar month. It appears around every 2 1/2 years and usually happens during a month that has 31 days in it.

Using Candles for Rituals

First, decide on the type of candle and color you wish to use for your ritual.

You will want to go over your candle with a cloth and some mineral or baby oil. You may also use lemon-scented furniture polish as it is the only scented mineral oil in the lemon oil and has excellent cleaning properties.

After cleaning the candle, wipe it dry. You may want to buff it to a nice luster if it appears dull or hazy.

You may also want to cleanse your candle with Florida water and smudge it with a white sage smudge stick.

Now that you have cleansed your candle, you may proceed to carve any type of symbol into it, any purpose you wish to manifest. For example, you may want to carve a $ sign for money or a heart for love or a house for a new home, etc.

You will now charge your candle by anointing it with any special oil to enhance and bring forth your spell. For example, you may use prosperity oil, good health oil, protection oil, love oil, etc.

In oiling or anointing your candle, remember, if it is something that you wish to manifest and bring into your life, you would want to imagine a triangle facing you, surrounding the candle, and pointing towards you. Then, rub the oil on the candle starting from the middle, rubbing the oil to you, and then turn the candle around and do the same on the other end, again rubbing oil towards you from the middle of the candle.

If there is something you wish to leave your life, then you want to rub the oil away from you, rubbing the oil on both ends of the candle from the middle away from you.

Matches are taboo on the altar because they are tipped with phosphorus and sulfur (brimstone), elements that release noxious fumes when ignited and are used in the black arts to invoke demonic entities. So, it is best to use a butane lighter when lighting your candle.

Birthday candles should not be blown out; you destroy the wish by doing this. Use a snuffer or allow it to burn out by itself.

By blowing out a candle, you offend the gods, and it destroys the spell for which you are intending.

Your intention is the key to manifesting what you want. Know what you wish to bring about in your life.

When burning the candle on your altar, if possible, have your altar facing north.

Steps for the Ritual

Sit in a calm place and get centered. Have your mind on the issue at hand and know what it is you wish to manifest.

Hold your candle in your left hand and with your eyes closed and in a meditative state, contact your angels, spiritual guides, higher-self, God and or the goddess; whoever you wish to help you at this time and say a prayer to them asking them to help you in bringing about this manifestation.

Now, place the candle in your right hand, and while focusing on your manifestation and intention, say, "This is what I ask for, and this is the divine right that I receive."

Now, place the candle in its holder and know that your intention and wish will be conducted. Thank your spirits.

You may now walk away. You do not have to think any further about the candle and your wish.

Let the candle burn itself out. If it goes out before it is fully burned, that is okay; the spell has been executed.

If you wish to do a banishing spell, or use the candle for exorcism, then you will need to bury the candle when it has burned out. Bury it in the far corner of your property.

Color Symbolism for Candle Magick

- Black is a great color for meditation purposes and psychic development. This is a good color to use for banishing rituals. It is also a good color for removing negative energies and when asking for a joyous outcome to a grim or impossible situation.

- White gives off positive, cleansing vibrations. It symbolizes purity, truth, sincerity, goodness, and the highest spirituality. This candle is good for all rituals to be used in a positive way.

- Red is the color of passion or any intense desire of any sort. It symbolizes courage, energy, radiant health, love, and sex.

- Pink symbolizes honor, gentleness, affection, togetherness, and spiritual fulfillment.

- Orange is for enthusiasm, fun, vitality, success, and bringing joyful things into one's life.

- The color gold brings good fortune, intuitiveness, peace, financial benefits, and promotes understanding.

- Yellow stimulates the intellect, imagination, creativity, skills, and sudden changes in the environment. It aids in the memory for healing. It helps to improve business and helps in bringing success in the performing arts. It is also a color for exorcisms.

- Green is the color for nature, material gain, fertility, abundance, good fortune, good health, and renewal.

- Light blue is the perfect candle for devotion, inspiration, peace, blessings, tranquility, immortality, faithfulness, fidelity, balance, and harmony.

- Royal blue is good for expansion and success in business and group enterprises.

- Purple is the color for royalty, dignity, wisdom, idealism, psychic manifestation, spiritual contact, and communication. This color is also used for psychic and spiritual healing.

- Brown is an earth color; it attracts money and financial success and all matters dealing with the material world. It helps us connect with the earth's spirits.

- The color silver removes any evil or negative influences. It stabilizes and neutralizes.

I have always enjoyed working with candles. When lighting a candle, it produces a beautiful warm and peaceful atmosphere. It has always helped me to meditate and connect with the other side in doing my spiritual work.

Candles can be used for scrying. By putting yourself in a meditative state and keeping the room dark, you can stare into the flame and sometimes see things about the future. You can also place a lit candle near a scrying mirror. Then after placing yourself in a meditative state, stare into the black mirror and that will help you develop your psychic abilities and see things you need to know. Candles relax us.

In churches, people often light a candle and then kneel and pray to God. When incense or candles are lit, the smoke goes up to the heavens and the gods are pleased. Always use candles to make your rituals stronger and more effective.

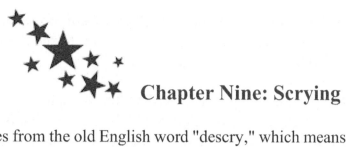

Chapter Nine: Scrying

Scrying comes from the old English word "descry," which means to reveal. When you are scrying, what you are doing is revealing the unseen and unknown.

Scrying helps you connect with your unconscious mind. All the scrying methods mentioned below require your ability to relax your mind, remove your ego, and focus on what you see. These methods may be easy for you, or they may require a lot of practice.

Always enlist the help from your guides and angels on the other side to help you with these scrying techniques. Record all you observe in a special scrying journal.

The most well-known person that did scrying was Nostradamus. He did his scrying by looking into a large pool of water. He added black ink to the water so he could see visions in the water, and he predicted the future with his method of scrying.

First, you may wish to smudge your area with a smudge stick made from white sage or sweet grass. You may also wish to light your favorite incense. You may also want to light a candle to put you in the properly relaxed environment in which to work.

Make sure you will not be disturbed or distracted from what you will be doing. You want your area to feel clean, special, and sacred. You now want to surround yourself with the golden white light from the heavens. And you may wish to say a prayer to your spiritual guides and angels to protect you in your scrying and help you in the process.

Various forms of scrying:

Wax-Take some hot wax from a candle, and let it drip slowly onto a water surface. When the wax dries on the water, you can see patterns to interpret and the messages that the spirits are telling you.

Mirror Scrying-Mirror scrying is done with a black mirror. Place a lit candle to the side of the mirror. Then, in your meditative state, you will relax while gazing and staring in the mirror, waiting for images to form so you can interpret them.

Water scrying-Again, you would put yourself in a meditative state and enlist the help from the other side. After being relaxed, stare into the water to see the future. You may use a black or clear bowl to do this.

Crystal ball scrying-After being in a relaxed meditative state, relax your eyes and stare into the crystal ball. When you stare into the crystal ball, you may first be aware of the milky, smoky, mist-like clouds in the ball. Eventually, the clouds will take on a color and you will see objects, pictures and images that will appear. It will be up to you, the person scrying, to interpret these images the best you can by using your intuition.

Fire scrying-This is an ancient method of relaxing your mind and staring into the flames. You will see visions in the flames

Chapter Ten: Automatic Writing

Automatic writing is a way in which you can communicate directly with your spirit guides, loved ones, or angels on the other side. Your guides communicate their messages to you through your writing. They do this by guiding your hand and pen. To benefit from automatic writing, you must practice it often. This is a method of communicating with the other side that takes a great deal of practice.

It's important that you don't have unrealistic expectations and immediate results on the first try. You may wish to light a special candle or your special incense to relax you and put you in a receptive mood.

It is essential that you quiet your mind and put yourself in a meditative state. Make sure you have removed the ego from your mind.

You must trust in the concept and the process as well as have faith that your guides will help you succeed in directly communicating with them.

The Steps to Automatic Writing are as follows:

First, you must choose and buy a notebook that you use only for your automatic writing. This will be a special notebook or journal that feels spiritual to you.

Second, make sure that all your automatic writing communication messages are in that one special book and not on various pieces of paper.

Third, once you have your special book and a pen in your hand, you are ready to start your automatic writing session. Before beginning, it is recommended to write the day of the week, time, and date on the top of each page to document the process. This will help you in understanding how well, how successful, and how effective you will become in both receiving and understanding the communication from your guides.

Fourth, figure out the best time of the day for you to commit to being in a meditative state to do your automatic writing. Plan to do this at the same time every day and in the same place. It needs to become a daily habit for you to become successful at this.

When you are ready to begin your automatic writing session, you will need to enter your meditative state where your mind is quiet, and your vibrational energy is high.

You may put a question on the top of the page that you wish for your guides to answer for you.

Then, start your session by first putting the date on the top of your page next to your question, and then address your guides and thank them for being with you today. Surround yourself and your guides with the loving gold white light.

Ask your guides if they will communicate with you through your pen and notebook today.

Now, hold your pen lightly and straight down on the paper. As you hold the pen in your hand, feel that loving energy flowing through you from the heavens, and it enters the top of your head going straight down your arms and out through your hands to your pen.

Ask your guides the question you have written on the top of the page and then just focus by going within and remaining silent. Allow your hand to freely write your answer on the paper.

When your session is finished, make sure to thank your guides for communicating with you and send them love and gratitude.

Chapter Eleven: Past Life Regression

Growing up in an Irish Catholic Boston background we were taught to just accept things the way they were and not to question anything. If they said you die and go to heaven, hell, or purgatory, accept this because this is the way it is. However, I always found myself questioning everything, but I tried to be a good Catholic and do what was expected of me.

When I met my neighbor Pat, she opened me up to the world of metaphysics and it really opened my eyes. One day she brought over some books for me to read and they dealt with the subject of reincarnation. I never really thought about reincarnation before. I always thought, "Well, one life is certainly enough to deal with!" I must say though, when I read these books, it was like a light went on in my head and I found answers I had been looking for all my life. What was funny was after I read the books, I started having dreams of my past lives.

The first dream I had was so vivid and was back in the early part of the 20th century and I had been a man and involved with a group like the mafia. Unfortunately, I had stolen some money from the people I was involved with, and they were out to get me, and this was in San Francisco. Although I had never been to San Francisco before in this lifetime, I could describe everything about San Francisco. Everything I saw was so clear. I remember meeting up with my sister and her husband in that lifetime and telling her I was in a lot of trouble, and she may not see me again. I explained to her about taking the money and that the mob were after me.

Well, they did catch up to me and put me on a ship that was docked at the pier. After brutally beating me up, I managed to escape and throw myself overboard. I remember drowning in the water. As I was drowning, this beautiful golden light came down through the water and these hands held me. It was God's light, and I felt a warmth and loving feeling I will never forget. Those hands that held me contained so much love it was unbelievable. I will never forget that incredible feeling.

Another dream I had, I was an old Protestant minister in a church in London, England. I had been a minister at the church for many years. I remember the church being made of stone and the time was in the 1800s. The church was also located on a street named Gloucester. There were woods located in the back of the church and the church sat on a low hill and had a lot of trees surrounding it. I loved being the only minister there and I loved the work I did; helping the parishioners of the church. It was a very fulfilling lifetime then. I remember seeing it vividly. I had that same dream two more times, so that lifetime was significant.

The other lifetime I remember is being from Ireland and coming to America during the potato famine. What happened was, during this lifetime, my husband, son, and I decided to go to New York City. We also decided to take the ferry over to the Statue of Liberty. While on the ferry boat I looked up and saw the Statue of Liberty and got very emotional and I just knew I had traveled there from Ireland, and it was very emotional, and I sobbed uncontrollably. I remember the feeling of seeing the Statue of Liberty and the excitement and emotion that moved me during that previous lifetime after traveling the seas for so long. Well, everybody on the ferry boat must have thought I was an emotional nutcase.

I also had three dreams of being a captain on a ship and going down on that ship. It appeared to me to be a fishing vessel. It was a hard life, but I loved it.

These past lifetime dreams reinforced my belief in reincarnation. These dreams were so vivid, so real, and struck a chord within me.

Past life regression therapy is based on the theory of reincarnation. Reincarnation is Latin for "entering the flesh again."

You are an accumulation of all the many lifetimes you have lived. These feelings and experiences are with you even today and although you may not remember them, they helped make you who you are today.

Reincarnation used to be one of the fundamental teachings of Christianity. Roman emperor Justinian had decided it would be much easier to control people if they believed there was only one lifetime to live, and then you go to heaven or hell. He went to Constantine in 553 A.D. and pressured the church to change its teachings and had Constantine state there was no such thing as reincarnation. It was after that that all the information regarding reincarnation was removed from the Bible.

Before I take you through a past life regression, I am going to direct some questions to you, and I want you to think about these things because they all relate to past lives. Ask yourself:

- Do you find yourself drawn to a certain historical time?

- Are you fascinated with a particular geographical area or settings?

- Are there any historical periods that you liked or disliked?

- Do you love living in the country, or would you prefer living in the city?

- Do you like the hustling fast pace of city life, or do you like the quiet peaceful country way?

- Do you like high-rise buildings, or do you long for wide-open spaces?

- Do you have the urge to live by water or mountains?

- Do you like or dislike chilly weather or hot weather?

- Do you feel déjà vu in any location?

- Are you drawn to certain cultures, ethnic groups, or ethnic foods?

- Do certain paintings, sculptures, artwork, or artifacts haunt you?

- Do you have certain feelings when you look at paintings?

- Does certain music tug at your heartstrings?

- Do certain sounds affect you, such as American Indian chants, African drum beats, Latin dancing, or ballet? How about folk music, or country-western dancing, or ballroom dancing?

- Are there certain tastes you like in fashion, jewelry, home decorations that you are drawn to?

- What about certain styles of dress? Do you like the prairie look, cowboy look, sporty look, intellectual look or the roaring 20's? What type of clothes do you like?

- What architectural styles do you like?

- How do you like to dress up at Halloween?

- Any particular type of costumes you'd like to wear?

- What type of movies or books resonate to you?

- Do you like movies that are adventurous, murder mysteries, tearjerkers, or comedies?

- Do you like war movies, or movies of medieval times?

- Do you like certain designs in costumes in the movies?

- Do you like romance novels like Jane Austen or the Brontë sisters?

- What about careers, what type of careers have you enjoyed?

- What classes did you enjoy, and what classes came easily for you?

- Do you have an ability, talent, or sport that came naturally to you?

- Is there a pattern in your relationships such as victim, victor, or caregiver?

- Have you constantly had money problems?

- Do relationships or career advances come easily to you?

- Do certain smells, sounds, tastes, touches, sights, prompt an emotional reaction or past life remembrance for you?

- Have you had any illness or pain, and you do not know the cause?

- Do you have birthmarks?

- Do you have fears? Fears such as drowning, flying, phobias of animals, fears of death, fears of childbirth?

- Do you have a problem with losing or gaining weight?

- Do you have a physical reaction to historical or certain places?

- Do you have allergies or addictions?

- Do you have recurring dreams or daydreams? Dreams in which you remember the details when you awake?

- Have you had Déjà vu where certain places or circumstances felt strangely familiar?

- Have you done or said the same things with the same person before actions occurred or words were spoken?

- Have you experienced strong feelings for someone you just met? Good or bad, love or hate?

- In your relationships, do you feel as though you've had different roles in past lives with that same person?

- Do you like or dislike groups of people?

These are all questions that you may have and when you do a past life regression you will find your answers.

Past life regression is a technique that uses hypnosis to recover memories of past lives or incarnations. Hypnosis is the state of focused attention bypassing the critical factor of the human mind and heightens susceptibility to suggestions. It is a process, a journey, which you take with the help of a therapist. You are in the driver seat and the therapist is your navigation system.

Since I am a certified hypnotherapist, I am going to put you through a past life regression. So, set your intention to enter the lifetime that is related to the issues you are working on in this present lifetime.

You may record this on your phone and listen to it as often as you like so you can tap into other lifetimes as well. This is a past life guided meditation. Each time you do this, you will be taken to a different lifetime. Give yourself time to understand your past life experiences and how they may have an impact on your present lifetime. What you experience in this past life, you will remember every detail about it.

You can write in detail everything you experienced after this regression. I hope you enjoy your experience and that it gives you peace. If at any time you wish to stop, just slowly and gently open your eyes.

Now get yourself in a comfortable spot lay, your hands gently on your lap, and close your eyes. Place your feet on the floor and take your shoes off if you wish. There is nothing to fear, you are divinely protected.

Now, to the count of four, take a deep breath into your nose. Slowly and gently breathe out to the count of five through your mouth. Do this again. Every time you breathe in, you breathe in peace and love. Every time you breathe out, you let go of tension and stress. As you breathe out your tension, watch it float away in the distance.

Again, breathe slowly into your nose to the count of four, and slowly and gently breathe out through your mouth to the count of five.

As you focus on your breathing, allow any thoughts you may have to just float away as you become increasingly relaxed.

Going deeper into Relaxation, one last time, breathe slowly in and exhale slowly out. Drifting downward into deep, deep, relaxation. Now, bring your breath back to its natural state and relax.

Now, just relax for a few moments, sitting peacefully and quietly. You feel so peaceful now, so relaxed, and so calm.

Pause a minute

Now imagine roots growing out from the soles of your feet and they almost look like the roots of the tree. Watch your roots going down, deep down into the ground, pushing their way deep down within mother earth. You can feel your roots going deeper and deeper pushing your roots deeper and deeper into mother earth. Mother earth welcomes you with love and she is giving you loving energy. As you move your roots deeper and deeper, you feel the loving vibration of the earth.

Now, visualize a brilliant golden white light around your entire body. This beautiful golden-white light is above your head and beneath your feet. See yourself cocooned in this wondrous energy and beautiful light. Feel how alive you are and how vital. You are warm and safe. You feel so warm and so comfortable, sitting in this glorious light, feeling the energy, feeling the vibrations. So peaceful, so relaxed, and so calm. Nothing will disturb you from this peace and relaxation. No distractions around you will interrupt you. Always remember you are safe, you are loved, and you are always protected.

Pause a minute.

Feel your body giving up all tension, you are becoming increasingly relaxed. You are more calm and peaceful.

Starting with your feet, you feel aware of the relaxation from the bottom of your feet moving up to your ankles. That peacefulness flows up from your lower legs up to your thighs and into your hips. You can feel this peaceful wave of beautiful relaxation as it moves gently through your body. You can feel your muscles become more loose and softer as this wave travels through you.

You feel pure relaxation as it flows through your pelvic area and into your abdomen. It is warm and relaxing, so calm and so peaceful. Feel this relaxation as it moves into your chest area, bringing with it such peace and serenity. Feel it flowing through your back and over your shoulders.

This gentle wave of relaxation moves through your upper arms, your elbows, and down into your lower arms. It tingles as it enters your hands, and you feel so calm and so relaxed. This wave of tranquility moves into your neck, the back of your head, and now your face. Feel it now flowing up to the top of your head. Your whole body is now filled with this beautiful, calm oasis of serenity. Allow your entire body to feel completely at peace and just relax.

Pause another minute.

You continue to breathe slowly and gently and feel at peace and relaxed. Your mind is clear as you go deeper and deeper to relaxation.

You now find yourself in a beautiful white room. The floor and walls are colored white, and the floor is also covered in a beautiful variety of colored rose petals. You can smell their floral scents.

You continue to walk through to the back of the room where there is a beautiful flame of a pink candle burning on a beautiful white draped altar. Next to the candle is a beautiful clear crystal and you can pick it up with your hand and walk to the back of the altar while holding the crystal. As you look into the crystal, you may see images in your mind's eye. Do not try to make any meaning in what you are visualizing or try to understand what you see in the crystal, simply observe it and let it go. You may feel or sense things, but you will feel at peace, calm and totally relaxed.

You now place the crystal back on the altar. You now find yourself on your own private beach and you can see a magickal forest off in the distance. You know you are in a place that is safe and happy. It is a place that brings you absolute peace and joy. You feel totally deeply relaxed. You have never felt so much peace, felt so calm and felt so relaxed.

As you stand at the edge of the water at the beach, you can hear the seagulls flying about and the sounds of the ocean. You feel the soft, warm sand beneath your feet. It feels just like heaven!

You now stand by the magickal forest, look around you, and see beautiful, majestic trees. You can see their branches sway gently in the breeze. You can hear the birds flying from tree to tree. And you can also hear the birds singing their beautiful songs. It is a gorgeous day, and the sun is shining on your face, and is warm on your skin. The sky above the trees is the most beautiful blue you have ever seen with only a few fluffy white clouds floating by.

Now, look around you, what else do you see? Do you hear anything else? You find yourself walking on an old, familiar path that you have walked many, many times before. The ground beneath your feet, is it grass, sand, stones, dirt, or concrete? You decide.

Feeling so calm, so peaceful and so relaxed, you start to walk along this path and as you do, you notice there are flowers along one side of it. What kind of flowers are they? You lean down and breathe in the aromatic scent from each flower, they smell of beautiful perfume.

As you continue to walk, you notice a fork in which you can go either left or you can go right. You decide which way you wish to go.

Pause for a minute.

You continue to walk on your path, and as you do, you see a movement ahead of you. You recognize this creature as your animal spirit guide. You look deep into its eyes, and you know you must follow it wherever it may lead you. So, you follow your animal spirit guide down your familiar path to a clearing in the forest. In the clearing, your animal spirit guide has led you to a magnificent temple. Your animal spirit guides you to the foot of the steps to this magnificent temple. You walk up the steps of the temple and notice the large doors in front of you. Look at the doors and see how ornate or how simple they are. You open the large doors and step inside.

Inside the temple, your spirit guide is waiting for you with open arms. You can sense the love your guide has for you; they are like an old lost friend. And you feel that strong connection as you are reunited with them. Together, you walk down a large hall. At the end of the hallway, you come to a flight of stairs going downward. You prepare to walk down the stairs and each step will take you into a deep relaxation. Every step down takes you deeper and deeper into a sleep-like state. I will count you down each step.

- Number ten, you feel yourself relaxing more.

- Nine, feeling lighter and lighter.

- Eight, you are relaxing deeper and deeper.

- Seven, your whole body feels so much lighter now.

- Six, you can feel the wonderful warmth all over your body.

- Five, you're beginning to feel that your image is changing.

- Four, you can see clearly ahead of you now.

- Three, you begin to catch glimpses of another landscape now.
- Two, your feet feel different as though they are not your feet.
- One, you are now at the bottom of the stairs.

You feel completely at ease now, so peaceful, so calm, and so relaxed. Everything you see, feel and hear, you will remember, and bring it back with you.

- Now, look down at your feet. Are you wearing any shoes, boots? Or are you barefoot?
- Look at your body with your eyes, are you male or female?
- How old do you feel?
- What is your name?
- What kind of clothes do you have on?
- What time in history is this?
- What is the date? You will see the date, one number at a time. The first number is, the second number is, the third number is, and if there is a fourth number, see it now. You now have the year you are in.

Remember all of this.

- Now turn completely around and be aware of your surroundings. Are you indoors or outdoors?
- Where are you?
- What country are you in? Let the letters of the country come to you; first letter is, second letter is, third letter is, you now have the name of the country.
- Become aware of any buildings.

- If there are people around you, can you look in their eyes? You might recognize somebody that you know now, although their appearance may be different. You will know who they are in your present lifetime.

- How do you feel right now? Pause.

You start walking home now, walking swiftly towards your home. You are standing outside your home now. What does it look like? What materials is it made from? You enter your home.

- Are there people inside? Or are you alone?

- If there are people, who are they?

- What do you see around you? What room are you in?

- How do you feel right now?

- What are your daily tasks?

- How do you make a living?

- How do you spend your time every day? What is your profession? What do you enjoy doing?

- What is happening in your life right now? Remember this.

Pause.

You now move forward in time; it can be days, weeks, months, or years but it is the time of something important.

- Where are you now?

- Who are you with?

- What are you doing?

- How old are you right now?

- What events are happening? Remember this.

Pause.

Still feeling very peaceful, calm, calm, and relaxed. Deeply, deeply, relaxed. Allow yourself to go even deeper now. Deeper with every breath you take. As you continue to relax, take all the time you need to explore these events. Remember this.
Pause.

Moving ahead now a few more years in time. And it will be the time of something else that is important in your life.

- Who are you with?

- What is around you?

- What are you doing?

- How old are you now?

Notice what is happening and what is going on around you. What was important about this life you are experiencing? What did you learn?
You are feeling so relaxed, so calm, so peaceful. Allow yourself to go deeper now, so very deep. You now approach the end of that lifetime, and you see it like an outside observer. You will do that very slowly now.

Go to the time of your death, this is simply a part of life and nothing to be afraid of.

There is nothing that can hurt you in any way. Simply look at it like you are watching a television screen.

What circumstances brought about your death? Were you ill? Was it a natural death? Was it an accident?

Is there anyone with you?

What did you learn from this lifetime and why was it important to recall? Are you bringing back anything from that lifetime that would help you in your present lifetime? You will remember all you have experienced in this past life.

Now is the time for you to return to your present lifetime and I will count from one to 10 returning you to the here and now.

- One, you see the stairway ahead of you.

- Two, stepping up.

- Three, remember to carry the lifetime back with you.

- Four, your steps are becoming heavier as you ascend.

- Five, becoming aware of noises around you.

- Six, start to feel your own physical body again.

- Seven, you can see the top of the stairwell ahead of you.

- Eight, you smell the rose petals ahead.

- Nine, you are aware of your own body now.

- Ten, you are back at the white room near the altar.

You leave now and walk through the magickal forest, seeing the flowers once more, the trees, and the birds again. Take some slow deep breaths again. Slowly and gently through your nose and releasing through your mouth. One last time.

Whenever you are ready, wiggle your fingers and toes and come back into the room. Fully awake now and remembering all you experienced.

Chapter Twelve: The Study of Wicca

Although I am not a practicing Wiccan, it is a beautiful religion.

Shamanism has been defined as the first religion. Shamans discovered power through alternative states of consciousness in which they communed with the forces of the universe. Through various awareness practices, all their magickal knowledge was obtained. The Shamans were able to connect with spirits and deities, plants, and animals, and opened new ways of learning and growing in a spiritual way. Later, shamans advanced in using tools to facilitate these awareness shifts, marking the beginning of magickal rituals.

Shamans used drums, rattles, reflective objects, music, chants and dance, the wind, the ocean, fire light, campfires, and the moonlight. From these primitive beginnings arose all magick and religion, including Wicca.

Wicca has dropped the ordeal of pain and the use of hallucinogens used previously at the beginning of tribal ceremonies. They instead adopted rituals that included chanting, meditation, concentration, visualization, music, dance, invocation and some drama.

Wicca honors the Gods and Goddesses and reveres the earth. Witches are male or female. Warlocks are those who have broken an oath and have been ostracized from the community.

A witch is someone who uses magick in everyday life. Everyone has the ability to channel energy. When you learn to focus on your natural energy, you will know how to increase it, channel it, and send it out into the world. The earth is sacred and is the source of our magick, connecting it to nature.

Connection to the earth is the foundation of good witchcraft. Getting used to feeling the energy of the earth pulsing through everything around you will help you connect to it, and that is what is important.

The rule of Wicca is simply "Do what you want so long as it harms none. And do nothing that would harm yourself." Concern and love for our planet play a significant role in this religion.

You can become a witch through solitary study, study with someone who is a witch, or join a coven where you will be taught the religion. A coven is a working group of witches which comprises 3 to 20 people.

Witches do not worship or believe in Satan. Satan is an evil devil that is a Christian concept and plays no part in the Wiccan religion. Plenty of books will give you a complete history of Wicca, but you can study these on your own.

Your book studies would include the Celts, the Druids, and the burning times in Europe.

In 1604, witches were hung in England, and in 1692, witches were hung in Salem, Massachusetts.

In 1986, the Fourth Circuit Court of Appeals ruled that Wicca is a religion and deserves First Amendment protection.

The three stages of a woman's life are the maiden, the mother, and the crone, and the three stages of a man's life are the prince, the king, and the elder.

The energies in Wicca are the Goddess who represents the night and faces the direction of the moon. And the God who represents the morning and faces the direction of the sun.

Wicca Tools for Your Altar and Ceremonies

Below are the magickal tools that you place on your altar and use during your rituals:

- Statues of a deity: Gods or Goddesses, for example, Aphrodite, Gaia, Isis, Pan, Diana, deities from the Greek, Roman, Egyptian, and Celtic cultures.

- Athame: This is a double-edged knife 6 inches long used to cut herbs. The athame is also used to cast a circle and open it. It is also used to invoke and banish certain energies and cut energy cords. I have used a letter opener as my athame.

- Book of shadows: which is your own personal book. You use this book to record your spells, dreams, magickal information, chants, etc.

- Broom: Use this for sweeping the area and purifying it, whether indoors or outdoors. Only use this special broom for your rituals.

- Cauldron: This object represents the womb of the goddess. It is used for cooking and brew making.

- Chalice: These are fancy cups or mugs used in our rituals as we drink beverages such as wine.

- Incense: This represents the element of air. You can use sticks, cones, or powder on charcoal discs. You may also burn your incense in a sensor or special container.

- Pentacle: This is the symbol of the Wiccan faith. It is an instrument of protection, meaning spirit rules over matter. It is represented by the 5 points, which are the elements of air, earth, fire, water, and spirit.

- Wand: This is used to direct the energy and to draw magickal symbols.

- Bell: Ring this object to bring in the four directions and the God and Goddess to join you during the ritual. Ring the bell at the end of the ritual to let the elements return to their realms. It is also rung to ward off evil spirits in spells or to invoke good energies.

- Divination Tools: These can be tarot cards, runes, pendulums, crystal balls, scrying mirrors, crystals or stones, framed pictures, or photos to be placed on your altar.

Also, place on your altar:

- Fresh flowers or herbs, God and Goddess candles, a snuffer, a lighter, salt and water containers, plates for cakes, cups for wine for everyone, cord, rope, sea salt, or chalk for drawing the circle.

- A special ceremonial robe for the ritual.

- A special altar cloth to go on the table.

- Wine or juice.

- Special cakes.

The Four Elements

Because witches believe that life itself is sacred, they also believe that anything that sustains life is holy.

The four basic elements to sustain our lives are air, fire, water, and earth. Wiccans believe that life begins when all four elements meet and combine their energies.

We need air to breathe, water to drink, the earth beneath our feet, and the warmth of fire to exist.

The mystical power of the air is knowing because it represents our thoughts, wisdom, powers of the mind, and our communication.

The mystical power of fire represents strong will and energy because it represents our passion and drive. It can bring about new life or destroy the old and worn-out one.

The mystical power of water represents healing, cleansing, and purification because it represents our dreams, emotions, and visions.

The mystical power of the earth is the wisdom of silence because it represents our ability to be realistic and practical. The earth is nurturing and stable.

It is important to learn how to transform into each of the elements in order for you to gain complete mastery of the elemental world. Focusing your attention for an extended amount of time on each of the elements will help you in your ritual magick. Learning to focus through the practice of meditation will also help you to achieve your goals.

- The air is represented by incense.

- The fire is represented by candles.

- The water is represented by water or oil.

- The earth is represented by salt.

Altar

Place your altar in the north part of your circle, or in the east, or the center of the circle. The north is the direction of power and is associated with the earth. However, some people place their altars facing east where the sun and moon rise. Other people feel comfortable putting their altar in the center of the circle.

The left half of the altar is usually dedicated to the Goddess. Tools that are sacred to her are placed there: the cup, the pentacle, the bell, the crystal ball, and the cauldron. You may want to lay a broom against the left side of the altar. The candle representing the Goddess should be on the left rear of your altar, and the color should be white or silver.

The right side of your altar represents God. A yellow or gold candle or an appropriate statue figure should be placed there. The tools that are sacred to him are the wand, the athame, and the white-handled knife.

Place the incense burner or censer between the candles and an offering bowl or plate in front of the censer. The smoke from the censer is offered up to both the Goddess and the God. Behind the censer, you can place fresh flowers, crystals, herbs, etc.

Wicca: Preparing for the Ritual

A Wiccan ritual is a means of creating consecrated, sacred ground or a sacred space to celebrate and strengthen our relationships with the God, the Goddess, and the earth. This ritual is also used to do magick and to work with the energy of the deities. The Wiccan ritual consists of a set of actions that are performed in a particular order.

People perform rituals for the same reasons they go to church. Rituals are special and give a feeling of being sacred. They create order and harmony in one's life and are a way to nurture and heal oneself.

Avoid participating in a ritual when you are sick, as it demands a lot of your energy. It is also not a good idea to do a ritual when you are very tired or in a hurry, as it needs your undivided attention.

Most importantly, make sure you won't be interrupted during your religious or magickal rite. If you are alone, take the phone off the hook, lock the doors, and pull the blinds if you wish. This is a very private ceremony.

First, it's important to take a ritual bath or shower. As you are cleansing yourself, you wash away all stresses and tensions which you have accumulated in your normal activities. Just imagine washing away the negative energies with the pure clean water. You can burn candles and incense in the bathroom if you wish. Fragrant oils or herbal sachets can be added to the water.

Outdoor rituals near the ocean, lakes, or streams, can begin with a swim. Once you are bathed, if you decide to put on clothing, the materials should be natural such as cotton, wool, or silk. You can perform your ritual sky clad if you wish, being nude under the sky. You may want to use one robe for ritual and keep it special for that occasion.

Before doing your ritual, you may take a magickal name for yourself. Your magickal name is also the name that other members of the pagan community will call you and the name the Goddess will know you as. The name should have some real significance to you.

Performing the Ritual

1. Sweep away all negative energies and cleanse your space with the broom.

2. Set up your altar in the center of your circle space and place your ritual tools upon it.

3. Place your incense on the charcoal, in the censer, or on the ashtray, and place it on the altar and light it.

4. Place your bottle of wine or juice on the altar.

5. Place your plate of cakes on the altar.

6. Put your candles in each quarter (north, south, east, and west), and light them. The yellow candle should go in the east, the red candle in the south, the blue candle in the west, and the green candle in the north.

7. Use your athame and cast your circle by drawing it with the athame. Make sure you cast it as a deosil, meaning clockwise.

8. Using the tip of the athame, draw up three scoops of salt, put them in the water, and stir them.

9. Now, take the salt water with your fingers and sprinkle it around the edges of the circle and on the members of the circle.

10. Carefully walk around the circle with the incense, waving the smoke from the incense everywhere.

11. Take the athame and go to each quarter, drawing the invoking pentagram in the air in front of you, saying, "Welcome, power of the east, power of the air, join us this night," or "I summon the power of the east to join and protect our circle." Do this for each quarter: the east, which is air; the south, which is fire; the west, which is water; and the north, which is earth.

12. Now, it is time to call in the God and Goddess. Light the Goddess candle, stretch your arms upward, and say, "Great Goddess, Mother of all things, Lady of the Moon, grace our ritual with your presence here tonight."

13. Then, light the God candle, and with your arms outstretched upward, you would say, "Great God, father, Lord of the Sun, Lord of the forest, Lord of the hunt, grace our ritual with your presence here tonight."

14. Say a circle blessing in front of the altar, "Great God and Goddess, I have built a circle with love. It is a holy place between the human world and the spirit realm, where we honor you and work our will. So, mote it be."

15. Do your magickal work, celebration, or Sabbat while stating your purpose.

16. Open the wine and cakes and bless them by holding your hands over them and saying, "I bless these cakes and wine in the names of the great God and Goddess."

17. Now, pass around the wine, and say, "May you drink the depth of life. May your cup overflow with love and friendship and may you always have enough for yourself and a friend, and may the bounty of the earth fill your table."

18. Now, outstretch your arms at the altar and thank the Great God and Goddess for joining, saying, "Great God and Goddess, thank you for joining us and blessing our rite." "Hail and farewell." Now extinguish the candles.

19. Drawing the banishing pentagram, release each of the quarters by saying, "Spirits of the north, west, south, and east, thank you for attending our rite, farewell."

20. Go to the center of the circle with the athame and arms outstretched, say in the counterclockwise (widdershins) direction, "To all beings and powers of visible and invisible, depart in peace. May there always be harmony between us? Our thanks and blessings."

21. Pour the wine and take it and the cake outside in the garden and celebrate.

Wicca and the Sabbats

The Sabbats are the seasonal celebrations that the witches celebrate. They are the eight annual passages of earthly and spiritual energy.

- Samhain: October 31. This is known as the feast of the dead and Halloween. It marks the end of summer when the Gods die. You celebrate this holiday by leaving food out for your departed ones. It is also when the veil separating our worlds is the thinnest, making it easier to communicate with the other side.

- Yule: December 19-23. This is known as the winter solstice. On the darkest night of the year, the son is born, bringing warmth and fertility to the land.

- Imbolc: February 2. This is celebrated as the festival of light, candles, and torches.

- Ostara: March 19-23. This is known as the spring equinox. And it is all about renewed life and fertility, the return of spring and warmth.

- Beltane: May 1. This is about joyously celebrating life, love, handfasting, dancing, and leaping over the fires.

- Lithe: June 19-23. This is known as the summer solstice. It is the longest day of the solar year and a good time to communicate with fairies.

- Lammas: August 1. This is all about harvest festivals and tending and harvesting the crops and getting ready for the long winter to come.

- Mabon: September 19-23. This Sabbat is known as the fall equinox. It is the time for deep reflection and finding what motivates you. It is also the time to prepare for winter making jams and jellies, and wine.

The Esbats

- The Esbats relate to moon magick. These are the 12 to 13 full moons a year, approximately every 28 days.

- The Esbat is honoring the Goddess at night during the full moon.

- Drawing down the sun or moon is calling the energy of the God or Goddess into you.

- The blue moon is a magickal moon when you have two moons during the same month.

- Magick is what witches do when working with the elements of nature.

- Magick is what performers on stage do with tricks.

Casting Magickal Spells

The waxing moon is also known as the new moon or first quarter. This moon lasts for three days, during which you can draw things to you. It increases things you want, knowledge, bank accounts, and relationships. It is about initiation and growth, new plans, and new projects.

The full moon is the second quarter. This is time for magickal and psychic powers, completion, illumination, Psychic ability is strong, and it is the best time for spells of any kind. Cast your spell three days prior and during the full moon.

The waning moon is the third quarter. This is time for banishing, getting rid of bad habits, getting rid of bad energy, illuminating, receding, separating, losing weight, completing projects, letting go, and cutting herbs and flowers.

The dark, black, or no moon is the fourth quarter. This is the time to rest and not to perform magick. It is time for reflection on what has passed, spiritual guidance, and understanding.

Chapter Thirteen: Meditation

To develop your spiritual gifts, first, you need to learn how to ground yourself. Grounding yourself will help anchor you in the physical world in which you live. It allows you to safely travel and experience the spiritual and astral worlds. Grounding yourself also helps you get rid of energy that is negative and draining and not yours. That energy can be harmful if you allow it to stay with you. This happens a lot to people who are sensitive to the energy surrounding them because they absorb it. In grounding yourself, it will help you feel calmer, less anxious, and more confident as you follow your path.

Good daily exercises to develop your spiritual gifts would include:

- Practice breathing consciously by breathing deeply and slowly.

- Spend time in nature.

- Take Epsom salt baths.

- Exercise.

- Be aware of what you watch on TV, do not watch the news. Do not watch violent, horror, or gruesome shows. If the programs are not uplifting and are upsetting, do not watch them.

- Spend quiet time by yourself. Learn to love yourself and understand who you are.

- Appreciate all that you are.

- Develop and practice forgiveness and compassion.

- Be grateful.

- Develop and practice saying positive and uplifting statements to yourself on a daily basis.

- Eat well and be grateful for this creation of yours.

- Spend time with family and friends that are uplifting and positive. Be around friends and family who support you and make you feel good.

- Remember that life is fleeting and very precious, so enjoy it.

- Above all, love yourself and know you are worthy! You are worthy of all the great things that life has to offer.

Meditation for Connecting With Your Guides

Meditation is really the best way to connect with your spiritual guides. When you are relaxed and receptive to them, your vibration is raised to meet theirs.

This will be a guided meditation I created that you can record and use repeatedly. Focus on your breathing, breathing in slowly through your nose, and breathing out slowly through your mouth. Do this several times.

Then, imagine your feet growing roots and going deep down into Mother Earth. As your roots go deep down into Mother Earth, they draw up this beautiful blue energy coming up from below and deep within the Earth. This beautiful blue energy travels up through your physical body and fills your entire being. As this energy travels up through you, it energizes your chakras. As it enters your chakras, it spins and opens them up like a lotus blossom, and healing occurs in each chakra as it moves through them.

Your chakras then spin and open like a beautiful lotus blossom. This beautiful blue energy courses through you, and you can feel that love and healing are taking place. Feel all tension, stress, and anxiety leave your body, and it is replaced with love, healing, and peace. Your chakras are becoming vibrant, energized, and strong.

This beautiful blue energy travels through each of your chakras, then all the way up through your crown chakra and out into the heavens beyond.

As this blue energy connects with the heavens, the heavens send a beautiful golden white light. That golden white light comes down and enters through your crown chakra, mingling with the blue energy and creating a beautiful green energy filled with healing. This beautiful, perfect, green healing energy courses through every part of your body, creating joy, love, and healing in every area.

Now, see yourself standing at the foot of a staircase. You begin to climb up the stairs one at a time. See yourself climbing higher and higher.

As you approach the top of the stairway, you see a door. The door gets closer and closer, and then you are in front of it. In your hand, there is a key. Put the key in the lock on the door, and as you turn it, the door becomes unlocked and opens. As you open the door, you step across the threshold to the world on the other side.

You see a place of beauty that resonates deeply within you. This is your favorite place in the whole world, and you love being here. This is what you can truly call home.

Continue moving forward in this place. You see a lovely landscape full of green grass and a variety of flowers in every color imaginable. You now find yourself walking along a path and notice your surroundings and how wonderful you feel to be here.

In the distance, you see a figure moving towards you. This is one of your spirit guides. As your spirit guide comes closer to you, you become aware of their appearance and the energy they carry with them. Make a mental note of these feelings so you can recognize them when you return to meet with them in the future.

Feel the warmth of the tremendous love that they have for you. They are your faithful, loyal friends and are here to always help and support you. As your spirit guide approaches you, they greet you like an old acquaintance because you have known each other forever.

You both now sit down on a bench nearby. Ask your guide about the role they play in your life. You can talk or just be together, enjoying this beautiful connection. Your guide is happy to answer any questions you have. You are enjoying this connection and the conversation you are having together. It feels like you are visiting an old friend and catching up on old times. You feel the unconditional love they have for you.

It is now time for your guide to leave, but before leaving, your guide places an object in your hands, and that object has meaning for you. Notice the object that has been placed in your hand and think of the meaning behind it. It is not by accident that you received this object.

Before leaving, ask your guide for a way to connect with them daily. It may be an identifying character such as a name, a symbol, a sign, a color, or a feeling. When you experience this identifying character, you will know your guide is nearby. Thank your guide. You will remember those feelings of love that they have left you with. And you will also remember the message of the object they placed in your hand.

You now see the door in front of you that you entered before. Step forward through the doorway and close the door behind you. You know you can return anytime you would like to your special place or your favorite place and meet again with your spirit guide.

Step down the staircase, one step at a time, until you reach the bottom. Now, return to the chair you were sitting in. Become aware of your body, wiggle your toes and fingers, and open your eyes. You now feel energized and at peace.

Anytime you wish to check in with your guide, you can go back to this meditation. The more time you spend with your guides, the stronger relationships you will build and the easier it will be to connect with them and receive information. You can also call on them when you are doing meditation, mediumship, or healing work.

As you begin working with your guides, it can be helpful to establish or develop some signs or symbols so that you know the information you're receiving is coming from them and that you are on the right path. Just close your eyes and ask if this information is coming from them. Then, trust how it feels. You will know. The more you work with your guides, the more you'll find them showing up in your life.

Meditation to Connect with a Loved One.

Without going within and meditating, any true happiness or success is only temporary.

The only way to get to know your true self is through the silence of your inner world and connecting to the other side.

First, we will start by sitting in a comfortable place with no distractions or noises around us. You will concentrate only on my voice and your breathing. During this meditation, you will feel safe, secure, calm, and at peace.

As you focus on your breathing, you will breathe in slowly through your nose for a count of four, hold it for a count of four, then exhale through your mouth for a count of four. Do this several times. After, you will find your own natural rhythm.

Now, I want you to go to your favorite place, the place where you feel harmony and complete serenity, the place you love.

Now that you are in your special place, you will invite your loved one into your consciousness. Think of the name of the loved one you wish to connect with and let that name and thoughts of that loved one fill your mind.

Keep focusing on your loved one until a blurry feature starts to form in the distance. Focus your mind's eye on that blurred silhouette as it slowly moves towards you. The blurred silhouette now becomes the figure of the loved one that has passed. Watch as the facial features emerge. See the face of your loved one looking straight at you. They are happy and contented to see you.

Feel your loved one's presence as you see them directly in front of you. Embrace the warm, loving energy as it envelops you. Your heart expands with the joy of having them in your presence. Open your ears to the message your loved one carries with them to you. Listen to what they are saying to you. Your loved one whispers the words they have brought for only you to hear.

Spend a few minutes with them and visit like old friends during old times.

Ask them for a sign so you will know when they are near you, and you will know it is definitely them. You will remember the message they have given you as they slowly turn and walk away and fade into the light. You will also not forget this experience of meeting with them and how it made you feel. As you think of this message, take several slow, deep breaths. No matter how big or small the message was, appreciate the fact that you were able to connect with them. You can connect with them whenever you like or as often as you like, and your loved one will always respond to you.

Now, you will take a few deep breaths and feel yourself coming back into the physical. Move your body, stretch your legs and arms, and remember all you experienced.

Chapter Fourteen: Chakras

Chakras are the internal energy system within our body. Chakras are like batteries that link the physical body to our auras. As they connect to our auras, they blend with spirit.

Chakra is the ancient Indian Sanskrit word which means the wheel, vortex, or circle. The chakras assist in keeping the connection between our mind, body, and spirit and help it to function properly. If our chakras are out of alignment and not in complete balance, our physical health can suffer as a result. When our chakras are in perfect balance and in harmony, they will spin in their associated color and open like a beautiful lotus blossom.

1st Chakra - Root or Base Chakra. Located At the Base of the Spine.

- Color- Red
- Crystals-garnet, ruby, red jasper.

This chakra keeps your body grounded and connected to the earth. It also relates to the feeling of stability, security, and our fight or flight reactions to situations. It deals with our basic needs. The first chakra, the root chakra, is all about making sure our physical needs are met; food, water, money, shelter, safety, and survival instincts.

Our base or root chakra is related to our physical body, which consists of our legs, feet, skeletal system, immune system, muscle tissues, and adrenal glands.

2nd Chakra - Sacral Chakra. Located Below the Navel.

- Color-orange
- Crystals-amber, citrine.

This chakra governs our emotional body, creativity, feelings, relationships, and sensuality. It is also related to our sexuality and our passions, feeling alive and feeling pleasure or pain. This chakra is also about our desires, personal growth, and our pleasures in life.

The physical parts of the body that relate to our second chakra are our kidneys, bladder, genitals, uterus, ovaries, and testes.

3rd Chakra - Solar Plexus. Located Just Above Your Navel.

- Color-Yellow

- Crystals- yellow citrine, gold topaz, and tiger's eye.

This chakra helps you to connect to your personal power, self-confidence, and energy. It is what gives you your gut feeling. It is about being comfortable in a group of people, self-worth, self-esteem, and assertiveness. This chakra is about your inner-knowing, guidance, and your psychic warnings, (which you will feel in your stomach area). The solar plexus is all about how we relate to the world around us, our personal power, and the power we have over our lives.

The digestive system, lower back, and pancreas are the physical parts of the body related to the third chakra.

4th Chakra - Heart. Located In the Center of Your Chest.

- Color- green

- Crystals- emerald, green jade, malachite, and green tourmaline.

This chakra connects your physical and emotional body. It is about feelings of love, giving and receiving love, empathy, compassion, forgiveness, and trust in others. The heart chakra is all about the love we have towards ourselves and others and our ability to love. Our heart chakra relates to how we release emotional pain.

The fourth chakra in the physical body relates to the lungs, heart, and thymus gland.

5th Chakra - Throat. Located In Your Throat Area.

- Color-Blue

- Crystals-turquoise, blue Topaz, lapis lazuli, and aquamarine.

This chakra is all about communication, self-expression, speech, and sound. It relates to talking and speaking the truth. The throat chakra is about how we express ourselves verbally.

The throat chakra in the physical body relates to your neck, shoulders, arms, and thyroid gland.

6th Chakra - Third Eye. Located Above In Between Your Eyebrows, The Center of Your Forehead.

- Color-indigo, dark blue.

- Crystals-Lapis lazuli, azurite, sapphire, fluorite, and sodalite.

This chakra is all about your imagination, your inspiration, your psychic ability, your intuition, your higher self, and your inner guidance. It is about your ability to see what is in front of you and your psychic vision. The sixth chakra helps us tune into our intuitive guidance and use of our gifts and what we know to be true. It is about confidently making decisions based on information we gained from our inner guidance.

The third eye chakra relates to the physical part of our body in our eyes and pituitary gland.

7th Chakra - Crown Chakra-Located on the Top of Your Head.

- Color-violet

- Crystals-amethyst, purple fluorite, clear quartz crystal.

This chakra gives you the sense of intuition, connects you to God, and gives you wisdom.

It helps you become one with the universe; it also helps you in the process of spirituality and enlightenment. It connects you to your higher self and the divine. This is the final stage of evolution of the physical body. The crown chakra is all about inner peace, access to innate wisdom, our connection to the other side. This chakra helps us be aware of our connection with all living things. Physically, the crown chakra is the central nervous system and pineal gland.

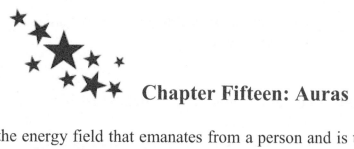

Chapter Fifteen: Auras

The aura is the energy field that emanates from a person and is their light body. All your love, hate, fears, pain, and your pleasures are reflected in your aura.

Some psychics and other sensitive individuals can see what is going on physically and emotionally in a person by studying their aura. All their thoughts generate energy, which is reflected in their aura.

Because energy is continually moving and changing, every cell in the human body will vibrate constantly with that energy. The aura is the energy around us that reflects who we are on all levels: emotional, physical, mental, and spiritual.

Auras can also be seen in plants and animals. In other words, all living things have auras.

Even inanimate objects have an aura because everything is energy. So, objects that are not living and breathing still have an aura but not as strong as a living one.

Remember, working with your psychic abilities is all about how you feel, not necessarily what you see or think you know. Therefore, if you cannot see someone's aura with your physical eyes, close your eyes, and you may see or feel it psychically.

Yes, psychic and energy vampires do exist. They are people who tend to drain our energy without us realizing it at the time. You may notice you become fatigued after spending a brief time with these types of people because they zap your energy and leave you weakened.

To be able to protect yourself, your aura, and your energy field, mentally visualize a beautiful white light surrounding you like a bubble or a cocoon, and that will prevent any negative energy from penetrating your auric field. Always surround yourself with this beautiful golden-white light of energy. You can always visualize a beautiful light of energy around your home, loved ones, or vehicle for protection.

After being around psychic vampires, cleanse yourself with an imaginary cascade of water flowing from above and over you, or you can take an actual shower. Then, see yourself being full of positive energy and vibrant with a strong aura. Visualize all the water containing the negative energy going down the drain.

Your Aura and Awakening your Sensitivity: Touch Sensitivity Exercise

Rub your hands together and then place your hands, pulling them close together and then further apart. You will feel that energy as you move your hands back and forth in this manner. It will feel like heat between your hands.

You can practice this exercise with a partner. Have your partner sit comfortably in a chair. Stand behind them about 6 to 8 feet or so and let your arms rest loosely by your side. Then, open your palms outward, focusing your awareness on your palms. Walk very slowly toward your partner with your palms open, and you can start to feel a slight tingling in your palms and fingers (although it may be very subtle). As you come closer towards your partner, you may feel a change in the temperature and feel a different energy, like you are pushing a bubble of air around them. Feel those changes in the different fields around your partner, and be aware of how you sense that energy.

You are feeling their aura. You can do this with your pets and plants, too. As you feel their aura, you can send healing to them.

Chapter Sixteen: Dreams

What are dreams? Wikipedia describes a dream as a succession of images, ideas, emotions, and sensations that usually occur involuntarily in your mind during various stages of sleep. Humans spend about two hours dreaming each night, and each dream lasts about 5 to 20 minutes. Dreams feel real because we use the same brain to process them.

Although dreams are mysterious, magickal, inspiring, and informative, it is not always easy to remember them. Usually, once we wake up and move, our dreams are forgotten.

Some of the ways we may work with our dreams:

- Keep a notebook, a journal, a pen, or a recorder that is easily accessible by your bedside.

- As you relax to fall asleep, tell yourself you will have a dream, and you will remember it.

- When you awaken, try not to move. Do not run off to the bathroom. Lay there for a minute and think about what you just dreamt and see if the memory of the dream is still strong.

- Write the dream down in your notebook. By writing down your dreams or recording them, even if they do not make sense at the time, they may make sense in a week or two when you read them over.

- If you are in a hurry and you do not have time to write down the entire dream, write down a few words to describe the dream. Just those few words may help you to recall it. You may also write down the feeling the dream has left you with. If you decide to keep your dreams recorded in a notebook, make sure you date the page.

My Dream

When I was in my twenties, I rescued a beautiful Irish setter dog. I called him Jeremy.

When I rescued him, I realized he had something wrong with his hip, so I took him to a veterinarian. He had had surgery, and they put a steel plate in his hip. This was before I rescued him, and now that steel plate had to be removed. The surgery was going to cost $600, and that was a large amount for me to produce that I did not have. That night, I had a dream that I was with my boyfriend at a bingo place. He had played the number 91153, and I had played the number 91154. When I woke up, I had the strong urge that I had to go play the lottery using one of these numbers, but I was unsure which number to play. So, I played my number 91154. Within three days, the number came out, but it was 91157. I won $600, which was the amount that I needed for my dog's surgery. Of course, I could have won one million if I had thought to add the two last numbers together, making it a seven. Oh well, at least I was able to pay for Jeremy's surgery.

Dreams are important because we can wake up with an epiphany or an "aha" moment. You may get an answer to a question you have been unable to solve. Or you may find a new direction to take. I believe our angels, spirit guides, or loved ones can guide us in our dreams.

I have had many visits from loved ones on the other side after they passed over. They were happy when they visited me in my dreams and told me so. My loved ones looked happier, healthier, and younger than they had in their last years on earth.

I remember years ago having a dream about an old boyfriend that I had still talked to occasionally. When I woke up from that dream, I thought to myself that I needed to call him and see how he was doing. It had been a while since we talked. That evening, his mother called me, telling me he had drowned in a car accident. He had gone ice fishing with some friends, and the ice on the lake had melted more than usual. Once his truck hit the ice, it went down immediately, and they all died on impact.

Our loved ones can connect with us through dreams because our minds are not filled with that everyday chatter, and we are relaxed and receptive to their visits.

Before going to bed, think of someone you would like to reach out to on the other side and ask them to connect with you in a dream, and there is a good chance they may.

Chapter Seventeen: Developing Your Intuition

ESP stands for extra sensory perception. It is a way of obtaining information or knowledge by not using your five human senses. Meaning sight, sound, taste, touch, and smell; but using your mind instead.

We are all psychic. Those hunches, curious dreams, recurring thoughts, and flashes of insight that you experience come from within you. You can learn to interpret, control, and use them in a good application. Developing your psychic abilities requires training your awareness of the world around you. Meditation can help because it trains your mind to stop jumping around and helps you focus instead. Meditation reduces stress and produces an increased sense of tranquility.

To develop your intuition, try and find out where your intuition comes from:

- Do you get visual images? Symbols?

- Does your intuition come from sounds or the voices you hear?

- Do you get a body sensation? A feeling of being touched? A feeling of hot or cold?

- Do you just know something and do not question it?

- Do you see things in your mind, like a scene playing out?

We all have these gifts.

If you wish to develop your intuition, I would suggest that you:

- Meditate for 10 to 15 minutes a day.

- Become observant: Being observant is like being in a waking meditative state. Be observant of other people by watching them without judgment.

- What are they doing, saying?

- What actions and patterns are you seeing in them?

- What do you think they are thinking about?

- Are they happy or sad?

- What kind of energy are they giving out?

There are many tools out there that can help you develop your psychic abilities. I will mention just a few:

- Tarot cards or oracle cards

- The Runes

- Scrying by using crystal balls, wax interpretations from candle drippings, cloud gazing, black mirror scrying, water scrying, fire or flame scrying

- Casting objects such as seashells, bones, runes, coins, dice, yarrow stalks

- Ouija board

- Molten metal drippings in water

- Pendulum and dowsing rods

- Spirit art

- Tea leaf readings

- Palmistry

- Tuning forks
- Singing bowls and Crystal bowls
- Crystals and Stones
- Automatic writing
- Channeling
- Psychometry

Chapter Eighteen: Mediumship

Mediumship

I have studied with the best mediums, online and in person. I have studied mediumship at Arthur Findlay College in Stanstead, England, and at Lily Dale Spiritualist Camp in New York.

I have studied with: Lillian Suarez, Lou Ann Beecher, Thomas John, Tony Stockwell, Gordon Smith, John Holland, Janet Nohavec, James Van Praagh, Lynn Cottrell, Sharon Harvey, Robin Hodson, and Tina Escoto. These people are great mediums, and I appreciate all the knowledge I have gained from them. They are individuals and they have their own unique way of teaching and doing their mediumship. As you study and practice, you will find your own way of doing Mediumship that works for you.

The things that will help you develop your mediumship are developing compassion and feelings for other people. Feeling other people's pain and joy and being aware of what is happening to them in their lives. It also helps you be aware of who you are and get past your ego.

Meditation is important. When doing this, focus on your breathing pattern. Try meditating for 10 to 15 minutes a day. Meditation helps you learn to quiet your mind, sit, listen, and become.

If you join a mediumship group, it will act like a mirror to you. What happens in the circle stays in the circle. And if you do decide to join a circle, give what you get and then let it be. What you receive entirely depends on what spirit chooses to give you. Remember, you have good days and bad days. Keep attending your circle, and do not become complacent. You are a messenger, not a judge. Practice your gift with the intention of helping people. Always ask the spirit for permission to come to you and give you the messages that will help the sitter. Their presence is what fuels you. Remember to be kind and that we are here to help and love each other. And remember, with mediumship, it is not about seeing; it is about feeling, trusting, and believing.

In mediumship, it is important to learn how to raise your vibration to match the other side's vibration. Being on the physical plane, we are on different frequency levels than those spirits on the other side. To raise your vibration, fill your mind with higher thoughts. Do your best to be positive and compassionate and bring good things to these people to brighten their day.

You also must learn how to switch on and off to spirits. In switching on, find your own internal switch, and you can do this by saying a ritual prayer or visualization and journeying to a higher state or place. Breathing consciously also helps.

When switching off, end with a small prayer or visualization. After switching off, ground yourself. You can ground yourself by eating a meal, eating chocolate, or connecting to Mother Earth. Your space is your own. No one and nothing can enter that space unless you allow it, and this includes your spirit beings on the other side.

A true medium shows great trust in letting go of their own space and allowing a higher being to occupy it. Overshadowing is when you are linking with the spirit. Trance mediumship requires more commitment and devotion.

History of Mediumship

Mediumships have existed, in one form or another, as long as people have existed on Earth.

In 1000 B.C., the ancient Greeks consulted oracles for answers. The Romans called mediums "soothsayers" and often sought their wisdom for answers. Even the Bible mentions occurrences of clairaudience in II Kings 6:12, Mark 9:2-4 and Acts 9:4-7. In later centuries, European royalty called upon their personal mediums, known as "stargazers."

In the 1600s, the church outlawed mediumship, and only priests were allowed to communicate with God and spirit. Anyone else would be put to death if they were caught practicing mediumship.

Modern Spiritualism started with the mediumship of the Fox sisters. On March 3, 1848, Margarita and Catherine Fox communicated with the spirit of Charles B. Rosna through a devised series of raps and knocks. Mr. Rosna was a peddler who had been murdered and buried in the cellar of their house. The Fox sisters held demonstrations in Rochester, New York, and went on to travel extensively to spread the religion of Spiritualism.

The main objective of doing mediumship work is to provide proof of the survival of the soul after death and to help the bereaved come to terms with their loss.

The purpose of Mediumship is to bring healing, peace, and love to the people here from their loved ones who have passed on the other side. The Medium brings messages and guidance as well as information to the sitter that they need to know. The spirit may answer questions about the past, present, and future. These messages are meant to help the sitter move forward in their life.

Mediumship connects you to your divine self and helps you find clarity and understanding on your spiritual path.

Mental Mediumship is communication with spirits by telepathic means. The Medium hears, sees, or feels messages from the spirits and delivers this information to the sitter.

Trance mediumship occurs when the Medium remains in an alert but altered state of consciousness while communicating messages from the spirit. The spirit, or spirit, uses the Medium's body as a channel and often speaks, chants, or produces automatic writing through that Medium.

Physical Mediumship may involve loud rappings and noises, materialized objects, spirit bodies, and levitation. Physical mediumship can also materialize spirit bodies through ectoplasm.

Transfiguration is when a spirit's face appears on a medium's face.

Mediumship and the Clairs

Just as you use your five senses in everyday life to connect with the physical world as a medium, you learn to use your spiritual senses to communicate with the spiritual world. The word "Clair" is from the French word meaning clear: clear seeing, clear hearing, clear feeling, clear smelling, and clear tasting.

Clairvoyance is the ability to see spirits, see images, see pictures, and see symbols that are sent from the spiritual world. The visions that you see are in your mind's eye. Clairvoyance is the ability to see psychically. You may see images, colors, shapes, outlines, and pictures. To develop this ability, practice looking at an object or an image and then visualize it exactly in your mind's eye down to the last detail.

Clairaudience means hearing voices and other sounds that come from the spiritual realm.

These sounds can be words, names, strings of sentences, or music. They also can be songs or different noises that are produced by spirit. Clairaudience is your ability to listen to spirit.

Clairsentience relies on distinct feelings that the Medium gets when giving a message. It is more of a gut reaction, a clear and undeniable feeling. The Medium relays these messages regarding certain issues, offering a particular name or going to a specific person when delivering messages to a large group. More accurately, it is a simple feeling or knowing without a clear understanding of how you came to know this information. You will just profoundly feel the person's emotions. This information makes you feel something or gives you that gut feeling. The best way to develop your clairsentience is by practicing psychometry.

Claircognizance is the same as clear knowing. A complete knowing occurs when you grasp an entire concept the spirit gives you all in one moment. You know something without any logical reason behind why you know it. The message gives you a powerful sense of knowing that goes beyond logic. For example, you have a certain thought that someone is lying about something despite all evidence to the contrary. Another example would be you have a sense of knowing that it would not be a promising idea to accept a job you have just been offered even though the job seems perfect for you. With Claircognizance, you may have premonitions about things in the future to come.

Clauraugustine deals with smells and tastes perceived in a physical way that may come through from the other side during a reading or a séance. You may smell tobacco, smoke, perfume, flowery scents, or baking smells. Or you may taste sweet, salt, or anything that would remind you of a loved one that passed.

Sitting In the Power

Sitting in the power is the ability to stay still, put yourself in a meditative state, and focus on your breathing. By simply sitting in the power, you can acquire the necessary knowledge and understanding of the spirit world, which will help you blend your energy with spirit.

First, you should find a quiet place where you will not be disturbed.

Set your intention to open and expand your heart chakra, and you're aware of it, and this will help you attune to the spirit world.

Visualize a beautiful ball of gold and white light spinning and getting bigger and brighter and expanding outward all around you. As you blend your energy with spiritual energy, feel it surrounding and embracing you.

In this spiritual energy, you can build your power and vibration to match the spirit's vibration. Because the other side has a different vibrational frequency, you must raise your vibration in the physical world to the spirit world, and the spirit world must lower its vibration to make the connection successful.

As you feel the energy changing and growing, it makes you more aware and more sensitive to everything around you. Therefore, you can receive messages more easily by sitting in the power.

Chapter Nineteen: Mediumship Practices

When you do mediumship, you may use a special stone or a crystal that you program for your mediumship practice. Hold it while doing your Mediumship. It may be a clever idea to keep a journal for recording your experiences while doing Mediumship.

Before mediumship and as a daily ritual, it is important to cleanse and protect yourself. Remember, throughout the day, we encounter some negative energy in our environment and people, which is quite easy to absorb. So, it is important that we keep our energy high, pure, and positive.

How to Cleanse and Protect Yourself

You will cleanse your energy auric field by imagining your body surrounded by a beautiful white golden spiritual light, the God light from the other side. Visualize this color in your aura. Then, see your aura as strong, powerful, and impenetrable.

How to Ground Yourself after Your Mediumship Practice

When you practice grounding yourself after your mediumship practice, you will balance the spiritual and physical energy in your body. You will feel lightheaded, tired, disconnected, and out of sorts when you are not grounded.

You can ground yourself by connecting to Mother Earth. Take a moment to silence yourself. Stand with both feet on the ground and your hands facing upward. Take a few breaths and focus on your breathing to calm your mind. Imagine yourself like a tree, visualizing its roots going deep down into Mother Earth. Then, feel the earth's energy coming up through you and filling your entire being. You will want to visualize this energy as a beautiful blue light coursing through your entire body.

You can also ground yourself by eating chocolate or food after your mediumship. You may also take a salt bath, which grounds you and detoxes you after your practice. Salt has natural healing properties. When you are grounded, you will feel clear and focused in the present.

To Shield Yourself

See yourself in a cocoon, a bubble, or a giant crystal, protecting you inside with a clear, healing, and loving light. The outside of this cocoon, bubble, or crystal is a strong barrier that cannot be penetrated with any negative energy.

Doing Platform Mediumship

Turn off all phones. Let go of the day and close your eyes. Play uplifting music. Spirits are attracted to happy and joyful music. Ground yourself with protection, the golden white light of peace and love from heaven.

You may now want to say a prayer to help you feel protected and help you make a connection to the other side.

Now, you will say, "I call upon my highest and most loving guides to be with me, to assist me, and to protect me from negative energy." "Thank you." Then, let the spirit know you are ready to communicate and allow them to come closer and closer. Your guides will always keep you safe.

Open your chakras and expand your heart light. There is nothing to fear, you are divinely protected.

Ask your guides to be loud and clear when they come through you, giving you clear and concise messages that you will understand and be able to deliver.

Then, say to them, "Please let me help them tonight. However, I may be of service." Let go of your ego.

Our guides are here to teach us and guide us. They inspire us. They are always positive, wise, and loving.

Spirits never waste a thought. Notice everything shown to you and give the information interpreted with grace. Do not ask questions of the sitter, just make statements.

Focus on spirit, not the audience. Trust your solar plexus and introduce yourself to the audience. Engage everyone in the room.

When taking a step forward, leave your fears behind. In your mind, say, "May God be with me and show me the way." Be aware of the moment and your spirits connecting with you.

You are receiving from spirit. You may ask your guides to put something in your hands, something that has meaning to the person you are connected to.

When you reach that perfect receptive state, you will become aware of the presence of spirit, and you will allow their energy to blend with yours. This is called overshadowing and is exactly what you want to happen during a reading or demonstration of mediumship. You want their energy to blend with yours making it easier to receive their messages.

Stay in your personal power. The spirit people know what you want, and they want to deliver. Once you feel you are in power, relax. Trust that the spirit people are not going to let you down. They want to make contact as much as you do.

Receiving and Interpreting the Messages from Spirit

Ask yourself the following questions:

- Is the reading physical?

- Pay attention to any sensations you are getting.

- Is it emotional?

- How compassionate were they?

- Is it mental, meaning does it feel intellectual?

- Are the messages spiritual? Were they religious?

- Some spirits do not want to talk about their passing because it wasn't as important as their memories while on earth.

Ask the spirit:

- Were they a man or woman?
- Were they old or young when they passed?
- How did they die?
- What was their relationship to the sitter?
- How did they spend their time in his life, and what did they do for a living?
- What did they look like?
- How did they dress?
- What was their personality and their character like?
- What did they enjoy doing?
- What are some of their important memories?
- Did they have pets?
- Did they live in the city, or did they live in the country?
- Where did they live when they were here on earth?
- What are some important dates to them?
- Can you describe family members that are with them on the other side?
- Were they in the military? Did they wear a uniform?

- Have them show you something that will touch the sitter's heart.
- Have them show you scars or injuries.
- Have them show you signs that they are around their sitter.
- How are they still present in their loved ones' lives?
- What have they observed recently around the sitter?
- Is there a significant date that the sitter would know? For example, could it be a birthday or anniversary?
- Why have they chosen to come through?
- And, what is the message for the sitter?

Can they make you aware of anything that has happened since they are passing? Anything that would let you know they are still conscious of life on earth even after they have passed.

- Ask for a special memory held between the spirit and sitter.
- Ask to see a death certificate.
- Visualize a clock for telling time.
- Visualize a calendar for months and seasons.
- In your mind, see the alphabet for letters when finding names and numbers for dates.
- You may see words, hear a song, and pay attention to your point of reference (things you are familiar with).

Be aware of how you feel physically while reading. Spirits may call attention to certain parts of your body to provide evidence about a distinguishable characteristic in that spirit's body.

The more you can express what the spirit is sharing with you, the more the spirit will express to you.

The spirit may use emotions to indicate messages and to share feelings that you are relating to the sitter.

Spirit tries to use a frame of reference when giving you messages. We are all unique people with unique experiences and knowledge. Spirit uses your experiences and knowledge to bring through evidence, especially when an experience connected to spirit is like an experience you have had. There are times when you will receive information that immediately resonates with you, and you will know it. The purpose is to remind you to trust what you get. Suppose it feels right and connects to you on a personal level. In that case, the spirit is using your frame of reference to communicate through you to your sitter.

They can be showing you art, pictures, objects, or symbols.

Spirit may show you objects in your environment, mentally compelling you to notice something to relay in the message.

It is important to share every image and every story. Spirits will make sure what you are seeing is essential.

If you receive an image, give it to the sitter. Then, take a closer look at the image and notice the small details.

Pay attention to the music and sounds you are receiving. Sometimes, spirits can make you think of a certain song or give you a specific message through the melody or lyrics of that song.

Sometimes, spirits will focus on tastes and smells that often relate to identifying themselves.

Expand your knowledge base to expand your frame of reference in your development. This is an important tool that you can use to improve your mediumship skills. Learn about different cultures, study the different states, go to new places, try different restaurants and different foods, look at different religions, take a different route to work, and see other neighborhoods. Listen to new music and watch the Smithsonian TV channel. The more experiences you have and the more knowledge you gain, will give the spirit more evidence to bring to you.

It is important to develop your own symbolism with your spirit guides. One way to do this is to develop a list of symbols that represent a person who has passed.

There are four ways for a person to pass. They may pass through an illness, accident, suicide, or murder. You can establish symbols for these four ways of passing. For example, you may see a heart for a heart attack, a rope for hanging, and a car for an auto accident.

We must have faith, trust, and knowledge that we have the ability to deliver. As a Medium, you must use discernment and convey the messages clearly. You must keep an open mind and focus on what makes you and your messages unique. True mediumship is about making the connection with spirit and bringing incredible love and healing through to the sitter.

Trust whatever you receive in mediumship. The more you trust in yourself, the spiritual world, and your belief that communication between the physical and spiritual is possible, the greater your success in your readings will be. Trust you, trust in spirit, trust your guide, trust the process, and trust in God, and you will be a successful medium.

When you are doing the reading, keep your eye on the spirit, not the sitter.

If you feel as though you are losing the link with the spirit, reconnect by taking a deep breath, stepping back into your power, and inviting the spirit to come closer. Then, ask the spirit to give you another piece of evidence to reestablish the link.

You may ask them to show you that again, please. When delivering sensitive information, such as a person who has committed suicide, just tell the sitter that this person is claiming to be responsible for their passing, and that is all you need to say.

You do not need to get a name for the sitter to identify with the spirit communicator. The spirit is not concerned with their name because that is not how they identify with themselves.

You can ask the spirit for a name, and then, if you can trust it, give the name or initial you are receiving. You may see the name or initial clairvoyantly. To help yourself see the initial, in your mind's eye, see the letters of the alphabet. Then, ask the spirit to highlight a letter they want to show you. You might experience an image or symbol for a name. For example, you may see a rose for the name of Rose, or you may see a relative of yours with the name Rose. You may hear the name in your head. Sometimes, you only get the first few letters of the name, or you will hear a name that sounds like the name. Just remember, receiving names is not easy, and it takes time and practice. Spirit will also try to give you symbols for a name.

Numbers can also be important evidence in reading. Getting numbers in a reading is like the way you receive names. You would see the numbers lined up and then ask the spirit to highlight the important numbers.

To get a month, visualize a 12-month calendar and notice what month is highlighted by spirit. You can also ask spirit to highlight which part of the month is significant, the beginning, middle, or end of the month.

Factors to keep your ego out of your mind. Release all judgments about others, and especially about yourself. Do not let the petty things in life control you. Notice your thoughts and actions to ensure that they do not take you away from your own spirit.

Be sure to ask spirit for what you need and expect that you will get it. As you continue to develop your mediumship, you will find that every Medium has his or her own style. What is so important to you is being yourself and keeping your own personality in your mediumship. You are also stepping into your soul self by stepping into your power.

When you finish the reading, show gratitude and appreciation, and thank the spirits and guides for all that has transpired.

When Doing a Private Reading with a Sitter

When you have a reading scheduled, you want to do everything you can to keep your vibrations high during the day. Be mindful of what you eat, think, and say. Also, be mindful of your energy, as you want to keep your energy as high as possible throughout the day. If you are having a sad or stressful day, call on your Joy guide to pick your spirits up. It would be best to reschedule the reading if you are ill or going through a very emotional time.

As you are sitting down with the sitter, explain to the sitter what a mediumship reading is.

Do your best to explain to your sitter that we are only an instrument through which spirit communicates and that we cannot control or guarantee who will step forward if anyone.

Then, ask the sitter to close their eyes and take three deep breaths. Breathing in through the nose and out through the mouth.

If you give the messages to the sitter and they keep saying no, just breathe through the situation and say, "I will ask you to think on this, and perhaps it will make sense with you or a loved one later." You may also tell the sitter, "Every message that I receive from the spirit is important, and the spirit does not waste words." If you hit a wall of noes, go back to the last yes.

Long pauses tend to kill the energy. When you are finished, thank the spirits for coming in and thank your sitter. A good medium will look to light in love and see light and love in everything.

Gordon Smith, a well-known medium from Scotland, uses his CERT method in doing mediumship.

- C-Communicator: Man, woman, child, age, male, female, and physical description.

- E-Evidence: Mechanic, artist, names, hobbies, mannerisms, memories, geography.

- R-Return: Why are they coming back? Love, asking forgiveness, what is the message? Run your mind over the alphabet.

- T-Tie up loose ends: Asking for it to be given to me in a unique way, final words, or love, putting the messages together.

Chapter Twenty: Spirit Help in Connecting With the Other Side

A spirit guide is a being on the other side that is assigned to you before you are born to help you on your spiritual path. Oftentimes, our spiritual guide is someone we knew from another lifetime that we were close to, and they have chosen to help us in this lifetime. Their number one goal is to help you in your personal development and growth while you are in the physical world. You can think of them as friends, helpers, protectors, advisors, or healers. They will not interfere in your everyday life unless you ask them to and give them permission.

Your spirit guide understands you in a way no one else can. Their advice and help fit into your unique journey and development in the physical world. An excellent way these beings can guide you is through meditation, automatic writing, or through dreams.

Your spirit guides are with you always. Knowing that your spirit guides are around you may sometimes make you feel as if you are being followed. You may feel a physical sensation like a touch on your shoulder or a breeze on your face or hair, or you will just know they are around you.

Along with contacting your spirit guides for help, you may also contact your angels or archangels. They would be:

Michael who is blue and is a warrior. His name means "Defender and protector." Archangel Michael is the one you call on if you are feeling unsafe or need protection. He is also known for fixing broken things. Because Michael carries a great sword of light, he can sever unwanted energetic connections to the past or people you wish to be removed from your life. He provides you with love and assists with healing.

Gabriel is white and the messenger. Archangel Gabriel helps to keep you motivated and focused on whatever task you need to get done. Her name means "The strength of God." She helps us be more creative and inspires us, especially in the arts.

Raphael is green and a healer. His name means, "God heals." Archangel Raphael is the angel we call upon when our health is challenged. We call on this archangel if we are dealing with physical pain or if we have other bodily ailments. Raphael heals physical ailments.

Uriel is purple and is the peacemaker. He is the archangel who gives you brilliant ideas with fantastic insights. He also gives us emotional healing and helps us in life transformations. His main task is to assist you when you feel lonely. He can help you heal the past so that you can change your life and manifest what you want it to be. His name means "The light of God."

Metatron is purple and green and clears away any negative energies or beliefs. This angel is known for instigating change and transformations in our lives. He can help you with time by adjusting it to help you with project deadlines. He is known as a protector of children and extremely sensitive people. His name means "celestial scribe or recording angel."

These are just a few of the angels who will work with you and support you. In mediumship, you will contact your spirit guides, angels or, archangels, or loved ones to help you with your messages.

Our Spirit Guides

Because spirit guides have lived on earth before, they have the knowledge of what it is like to be human and that's what makes them great teachers. Their role is to gently guide you to stay on track with your soul's purpose. They will connect you with the people, experiences, resources, books, and whatever it is that you may need to help you reach your spiritual goal.

Your spiritual guides are here to help you. These guides may come in and out of your life based on your development and what guide you may need. Your spirit guides will also give you insight through your intuition.

You Have Your Main Spirit Guides, And They Are:

Joy Guide-They may sometimes appear as children or characters such as a leprechaun, sprite, gnome, or an animal. They try to bring out the lighter side of you by bringing a little joy and humor into your lives when you need it.

Protector Guide-They protect you and keep you from dangerous situations. Some of our protective guides have lived a physical life at one time or another in history and come from indigenous cultures that lived close to the land. They may have been Native Americans or skilled warriors and fighters, and they continue to use these protective energies and skills to help us from the other side. Because you may face danger every day, they will watch over you and give you divine protection and messages regarding your safety. They help you maintain your energy during your readings.

Doctor Teacher Guide-This guide inspires you to achieve your best and to reach your success you work so hard to attain. Most importantly, though, they are concerned with your spiritual development. You can go to your doctor teacher guide when you have spiritual questions, and they will do their best to help you find the answers you need. They have the information and knowledge to share with you. They try their best to keep your mind open to the spiritual possibilities that will lead you in the right direction. They help guide you in making the right decisions for your spiritual growth.

Doctor Chemist Guide-This guide is concerned with the physical state of your body and your well-being. They are interested in you maintaining a healthy lifestyle, so they watch over your food, drink, and exercise habits. They can help facilitate healing from their position in the spirit world. They strongly recommend daily meditation, eating well, and exercising. They will help you raise your body's vibrational energy as you develop your Mediumship.

Master Guide-Their energy is very high because they maintain a higher vibration. The master guide is very calm, and you can experience the beauty and love they emit. They support you and everything you do and send you love and help whenever you need it.

Gatekeeper-This guide oversees organizing the spirits on the other side who wish to come through when delivering messages while doing your mediumship. They carefully manage what spirits come through.

Messenger Guide-this guide helps you in how you wish to receive the information from spirit. They're able to help you with symbols that they know you will understand. Establishing symbols with your messenger will make the symbols you receive clear and concise.

By the way, the guides have made their presence known to you, and you will distinguish which guide it is. The guide will give you a sensation better known as "their calling card." This could be a special feeling, sound, chills, a change in pressure around you, subtle dizziness, ringing in the ears, a feeling of being touched, a particular smell, and many other distinguishable signs. You can ask them to give you a particular calling card sign whenever they are near you so you will know which guide it is. You may experience itchy palms, an itchy nose, a gentle breeze across your face, and other sensations.

Melding is when you allow a spirit to blend its energies with yours. Your body becomes the spirit's body. This may take time to develop and requires a great deal of trust on your part.

Signs

In life, your beloved team of guides communicate with you through signs. They show you signs to convey their messages to you. They use these signs because they want to guide you, support you, love you, and protect you. It is up to you, however, to pay attention to the signs you receive from them and then use the wisdom you have within you to correctly interpret those signs. When it comes to signs from spirits, believing is seeing. Your guides try to use signs as a way of communicating, guiding, and connecting with you.

Your spirit guides often show you signs from your loved ones when you watch television commercials, movies, and other programs. You may also get a sign by hearing your loved one's favorite song or music. You may also see license plates that remind you of your loved one who has passed.

Signs may also come to us through conversations with other people. A person may make a statement that would be quite common from your loved one on the other side. You may also receive fun signs when you find pennies and other coins on the ground. You may also receive signs of nature, such as hummingbirds, butterflies, dragonflies, ladybugs, and birds, especially if they fly near you or land on you.

Finding feathers can also be a gift from your loved ones. You may also see rainbows in the sky.

They can also send you messages of love through scents and smells. You may find smelling a particular scent reminds you of a loved one. An example of that smell may be their favorite perfume or goods that they baked.

Sometimes, you can look at clouds, and they are shaped in a specific way to communicate with you personally.

Another common sign that appears to you is numbers, especially repeated numbers. Your angels' way of letting you know they are always with you is when you continually see those same numbers.

How often have you heard your name called, and it sounded exactly like the voice of a loved one from the other side calling out? That is their way of letting you know they are around you.

You may also find lightbulbs that flicker, microwaves making noises, and other electronic devices that act strangely. These are also signs from loved ones.

You may have noticed a person who reminds you so much of a loved one who has passed, either in mannerisms or physical appearance. This is also a sign that your loved one is thinking of you.

And, of course, your loved ones often will visit you in your dreams. This is to let you know that they love you and are always around you.

Chapter Twenty-One: Healing

I am a Reiki Master and a Oneness Blessing Giver. I have studied both healing modalities and find them both highly effective.

The Reiki method of healing originated in Japan. It means universal life energy. It is a healing technique based on the principle that the therapist can channel energy from above into the patient. Using touch and symbols, the therapist activates the natural healing process of the patient's body and restores physical and emotional well-being.

The Oneness Blessing Giver uses Deeksha as a method of healing. This is a non-denominational transfer of energy from one person to another. It is a hands-on transference of divine energy that brings about a state of oneness or enlightenment. The hands activate the energy healing process by placing the hands above the crown of the patient's head (usually for about one minute).

Ho'oponopono is a traditional Hawaiian healing practice of reconciliation and forgiveness. The Hawaiian word translated into English means correction. Similar forgiveness practices are performed on islands throughout the South Pacific, including Hawaii, Samoa, Tahiti, and New Zealand. This healing helps purify one's body and eliminate unpleasant memories or emotions that keep one's mind in a negative state. It restores self-love and balance. This healing is about taking total responsibility for everything that surrounds us. In this technique, you talk to your God, your divine, or whoever you believe is your higher being.

Your inner subconscious mind is where you hold negative thoughts and beliefs. For example, money is evil, relationships are difficult, etc. These negative thoughts wipe out your conscious intentions, goals, and things you want to have in your lives. You need to get clear and remove these negative thoughts so you can have what you want immediately. When you get clear, you remove these blocks, remove self-doubt, and remove the things that sabotage your conscious goals and desires. People in the world around you are reflections of you and are always mirroring your beliefs.

The Ho'oponopono transforms you and your negative mind and helps you connect to the divine. You don't need to know what your blocks are; you can simply say these four statements, which I will mention in a moment.

Most of you are looking outside to change. This technique will clear your negative beliefs.

You are 100% responsible for everything you experience; you experience these situations because you are the common denominator. This healing comes from within you as it is all within you. You cannot change anyone or anything, only you. When you heal within, your emotions are healed. All beliefs you have about money, relationships, and health will be changed for the better.

When you say the statements, say them like a prayer to the divine. You do not have to say them aloud. To begin, think about what is bothering you, pushing your buttons, and what arises from within and upsetting you. Whatever is bothering you, it is something that you are reacting to. It is an emotion and a feeling. You do not need to know the story behind it, nor do you need to understand why; just understand that it is. This could be anything that is holding you back.

The healing technique is to close your eyes and call on your God or divine being. As you feel this emotion, pretend you are speaking to them in a genuine way. Say these four statements sincerely and from the bottom of your heart.

- Number one. I love you
- Number two. I am sorry
- Number three. Please forgive me
- Number four. Thank you.

This is all you need to do; you have now worked on your inside. Now, be expectant of the change on the outside of you. If there is someone you need to forgive, you can say this prayer to their spirit. By saying this prayer, you are releasing the blame on everyone and everything. You may need to forgive your ancestors or your lineage; this prayer will help. This method of healing will give you peace.

 **Chapter Twenty-Two: Susan Marie**

I remember being a teenager and sitting at the beach back in Massachusetts. As I was sitting on the beach, I looked over, and there was a group of deaf people who were young teenagers (about my age at the time). I was fascinated by watching them use sign language. They were having such a fun time, laughing and conversing. I was so impressed and engrossed watching their conversation, even though I had no idea what they were discussing. Little did I know that deafness would become a permanent part of my world.

In 1977, I was recovering from surgery and wanted to go on a trip before returning to work. I remember talking with my mother and telling her that I would really like to go somewhere before I had to go back to work. She told me that her best friend Alice, who lived in New Mexico, would be a great person to visit and that New Mexico would be a wonderful place for me to see. My sister Priscilla had been there before and really liked it, often saying she would like to move there. I called my sister up and asked her if she would like to go on a trip to Albuquerque, New Mexico. I told her I would pay her way, and we would go and have a fun time. It was arranged that we would go and stay with Alice.

So, we traveled to Albuquerque, New Mexico, and Alice was very gracious. Alice took us around New Mexico, showing us all the historical and interesting sites, and we got to know another part of the country. We also saw unfamiliar cultures, such as Hispanic and Native American. We experienced what life was like in the southwestern part of the country. This was an education. Everything was different than New England, including the cultures, the foods, and the weather. When we first arrived in Albuquerque, we got off the plane, and I remember how hot and dry the air was. I noticed that if I closed my hands, they would sweat, but when I opened them up, they would dry immediately. I also remember how strong the sun was and how it hurt my eyes to open them up. I had never seen such a bright sun before; it amazed me.

On the final day of our trip, Alice was having company, so my sister and I had to stay at a motel. We were at a motel without a car and no way to get around. Back in 1977, they did not have Ubers or Lyfts. They had taxis, but we were lost and didn't know where to go. After we checked in the motel, we noticed Church's Fried Chicken across the street, so we decided to get some lunch there.

I was impressed with the chicken and told the manager I thought it was good. We talked to the manager and engaged in conversation about where we were from and the differences between New Mexico and New England. As our discussions lengthened, he decided to take the afternoon off with one of his workers, drive us around, and show us more sights of Albuquerque. Normally, I would not ride with strangers, but this felt right, so we did. He did not feel like a stranger, and we had a strong connection. He took us around and showed us the beautiful parts of Albuquerque. At one point, we even went to his mother's house in the country, a beautiful large Hispanic-style adobe home. It was quite impressive with its balconies and courtyard. This was a home style you would not see in New England.

We drove up to the Sandia Mountains, which have the highest tramway in the world, and it was absolutely a breathless, remarkable sight as we looked over the city.

I just knew then that my life would never be the same. Growing up in New England, I used to think, "There must be a place where the sun shines, and it must be warm and beautiful." I really disliked the long, cold winters back east.

So, I went back home and got ready to return to my job and my regular everyday routine, but I could never get New Mexico or Juan out of my mind. At that point in my life, I was ready to have a family. I was tired of drinking and partying and was ready to settle down.

I had a boyfriend back East, but as much as I loved him, I could not put up with his addiction to alcohol and his everyday drinking. He would not admit he had a problem, so it became a problem with us. I will always cherish the great memories of our time together, but my life with Jackie was finished. His life was drinking and partying and being up in Maine, which he loved. I loved Maine in the summer, but in the winter, it was too cold for my taste. He was great; we loved each other, but sometimes, love is not enough. Because he would not give up the drinking, it was time for me to move on.

So, Juan and I talked each day for hours, and I knew my future was with him and in New Mexico. I just knew we were supposed to have a family, which is why we were brought together in this lifetime. He was to be the father of my children.

We married in October of 1977, and I got pregnant right away. When I found out I was pregnant, I was truly excited because I wasn't sure it would happen because of my previous ovarian cyst surgeries.

When I was told I was pregnant, I knew I wanted a girl—a very independent girl. And I got exactly what I asked for. Because my husband and I could not agree on a name, we named her Susan Marie, giving her a different middle name.

She was a beautiful baby girl with golden curls. When she was born, she didn't cry or scream; she just managed to make some little "coo" sounds.

When she was nine months old, my husband and I went to Boston to visit my parents.

One day, while my husband and I were driving around, my mother watched our daughter when she accidentally dropped some metal pans, making a loud noise. She noticed that when the pans hit the floor, making a loud noise, Susan Marie did not even flinch at the sound or react in any way. When we returned to the house, my mother told me we needed to have her hearing checked. I had noticed that Susan Marie did not seem to react to noise, but I just thought she was focused on other things that drew her attention.

At this time, my husband got transferred to Denver, Colorado. We went to Denver and made an appointment with the children's hospital there to have Susan Marie's hearing evaluated.

The doctors told us that our daughter had profound hearing loss. Being naive, I thought, "Well, we'll just get her hearing aids, and that will fix the problem." Unfortunately, that was not a solution. The doctors explained that the nerves in her inner ear did not develop and could not send messages to the brain. She could identify with deep, low-decibel tones with a lot of vibration, such as a train going by or the sound of drums.

However, because speech is heard at an extremely high decibel range, she would be unable to hear words spoken. We were also told that only 40% of words spoken can be seen on your lips. Therefore, lip reading was not as simple as it sounded.

Susan Marie began speech therapy at nine months old and learned sign language. At this time, we moved back to Albuquerque, where she began daily classes for the deaf at the preschool. My husband and I also started taking classes to learn sign language. Susan Marie attended preschool until she was six years old. Then we had to make the choice to either mainstream her in public schools in Albuquerque or she needed to go to the Santa Fe School for the Deaf.

Because we wanted her to excel in whatever activities and subjects interested her, we sent her to Santa Fe, where she could be successful and feel confident with her abilities. By going to school in Santa Fe, she was able to take extracurricular classes such as drama, soccer, and cheerleading, which she as great at. Another plus with her being at that school was the fact that she was with other children with similar disabilities.

When Susan Marie was home on the weekends, I knew things were difficult because she was around people who could not communicate using sign language. She would be loud and vocal, and people would turn and look at her and not understand the noises she would make. I always had to sign to her to turn her voice off in public.

We had a pool in our backyard, and she and her brother would have a fun time screaming and yelling. Unfortunately, my neighbors did not appreciate her behavior. They complained to me that I would not have any friends because of my children's outbursts and noisy ways. Some neighbors would go as far as not to allow their kids to play with my daughter. It broke my heart! My son learned sign language very quickly, and he was two years old before he could speak it because he enjoyed signing with my daughter. My son was born 2 1/2 years after my daughter.

Because communication was difficult, Susan Marie wanted to spend all her time with her deaf friends, who shared her interests and challenges.

Once, we were out with a co-teacher friend and her kids and went to a pizza place. We were all sitting at a table, eating and conversing, when my daughter started crying. When I asked her what was wrong, she said that everyone was talking, and she was left out of the conversations because she had no idea what was being said. This incident made me realize how isolated she felt, and my heart ached for her. They say that being deaf is one of the most challenging disabilities because you can be in a room with a group of people and have no idea what is being said and what the conversation is about.

I was so glad that my son was the best brother Susan Marie could ever have asked for. He always used sign language and made sure she was not left out and in the dark about anything going on. When my daughter was around her deaf friends, they had common experiences and things to talk about, and she did not feel shut off from the rest of the world like she did around hearing people.

All of Susan Marie's teachers from the preschool and the school in Santa Fe were outstanding in every way. I will always be grateful for all she learned because of them.

My children were God's gift to me because I learned so much and grew up because of them. Before I had my children, I was self-absorbed, and the world revolved around me. As difficult as it was (especially raising a very independent deaf daughter), it was worth it all, and I would not change it for the world. My daughter and I often locked horns because we were both feisty, strong-willed, and determined to have our own way. We were a lot alike, which did not make things easy.

My daughter graduated from high school in Santa Fe, took college classes, obtained her certification in phlebotomy, and then went on to work in the medical field. Along the way, she had three daughters. Susan Marie has always chosen to do things her own way. She is a beautiful and kind person and radiates with love.

Deafness has opened an entire world for me. I love and appreciate my daughter because she is truly awesome. Having a disability is not easy for anyone, and it helped me really appreciate what I have in my life and never take things for granted.

Our lives can change at any moment. But I believe everything in our life happens for a reason and that there are no coincidences. We signed up for all of it before we entered this lifetime; all the good and all the not-so-good. All of this is to help us on our spiritual path and help us be better humans while on the Earth's plane. We are all learning while walking our way home.

Chapter Twenty-Three: Pets

Because the pets I have had were such awesome, amazing, and loveable creatures, bringing so much joy into my life, I would like to dedicate a chapter to them.

I believe all animals have souls, and our pets always give us unconditional love. It does not matter if you have had a bad day and you come home and you're in a rotten mood and grouchy; those little animals come up to you and give you their love and affection and are totally sincere in doing so. Only those who have lost a pet can understand the heartache of losing them.

Pets teach us responsibility in caring for an animal dependent on us for food and shelter. They teach us to put another being's needs ahead of our own. Our pets can often protect us from dangerous situations. These creatures can see spirits around us when we cannot. They also can size up people and know if those people are good or bad.

We have a responsibility to take care of the creatures in the world. Part of our responsibility towards animals and creatures involves keeping our planet safe, clean, and unpolluted. It is also our responsibility to make sure animals are not mistreated or abused, such as being chained up, not being fed, left out in the cold or heat without shelter or water, not getting necessary medical care, or being placed in puppy mills. All people and creatures deserve to be treated well, with care and love.

Besides having parakeets while growing up, my first experience with a pet was Barney, our pet dog. He was the runt of the litter, and I remember when my parents first got him. He was so tiny, and his stomach would swell up as he drank the water. He was a sweet dog, and every Saturday, my dad would take him for a drive, and they would go to the dump together to throw the trash. We had Barney for 13 years.

I was living in Corpus Christi, Texas, at the time, and for some reason, I was thinking about having a dog in my life. I do not know why, but a dog was on my mind. One day, I pulled my car into the driveway, got out of the car, and looked behind me. There was this beautiful dog that approached me with his tail wagging. He was about 6 months old. I felt like I was getting a greeting from an old soul, and as he came over to me. I patted him and felt an immediate kinship.

This beautiful dog was covered head to toe with ticks. My husband and I bought medicine, washed the dog down, and removed all the ticks. I named the dog Chelsey; we have had him for 18 years. Chelsey was a Rhodesian Ridgeback which are known for being a family dog; and he lived up to that description.

Sometimes, Chelsey would escape from the yard, walk down the street, and explore the neighborhood. He was very smart and would come right back when he was ready. We also got a greyhound and named her Brandy. They had retired her from the racetracks. Brandy was a sweet dog but had a much harder time connecting with people. The Greyhound's bodies are abused when living at the racetrack because they are trained to race and chase the rabbit. The dog's owners at the racetrack will go to extreme measures to ensure the greyhounds will run fast and chase the rabbit.

We later moved to Moriarty, New Mexico. We built a huge pen in the back of our land, with some trees enclosed. The two dogs would stay outside in the pen overnight in the hot weather. Once, in the middle of the night, I heard Chelsey bark, which was quite unusual. I was too tired to respond, so I stayed in bed. The following morning, I went out to feed the dogs and give them fresh water, and I realized Brandy had died in the middle of the night, and that was why Chelsey had barked. Poor Brandy was prone to seizures, so she must have had one in the middle of the night.

After moving to Albuquerque, New Mexico, my son approached me one day with an Australian Cattle Dog. He said that his father had found it on the side of the road and that if he did not take it, his father would have to have it euthanized. Because my son is the most loving, kind, sensitive boy in the world and loves animals, he could not let that happen. One day, the dog was in the back of his grandmother's house, and his grandmother looked out the window and, while looking at the dog, said, "Did you get a pig? "The dog looks so much like a little pig in the distance that it was appropriate to call her Piglet. Of course, we took care of Piglet because my son had to work so much. And Piglet lived to eat. That was the whole purpose of her existence: to eat, eat, eat. But Piglet also loved to please people.

My cousin Lee adopted a five-year-old Lhasa Apso dog named Tashi. Lee had the dog for a few years, and then Lee developed COPD. She became very ill, and about a year before she died, Lee asked if we would take Tashi. I always loved Tashi and would often take her for walks when my cousin could not. So, we welcomed Tashi into the family. Tashi was a very independent and particular dog. I would describe her as a princess because she always liked things her way. We had Tashi for about 6 years, and during that time, she became blind in one eye, deaf in one ear, and had had a tumor on her forehead for over a year. She kept going strong until she passed at about 17 years of age.

My son also adopted another dog called Mocha. Mocha was so attached to my son, and they seemed like soulmates. No matter where my son would walk, Mocha would just walk by his side without a leash and stick by my son's side like glue. She loved being around people and was lonely while my son worked. So, we kept Mocha at our house.

Mocha was just full of love. She looked like a brown Labrador but with a stance like a pit bull. Sometimes, I would take Mocha's head, hold it in my hands, and look into her eyes. I would talk to her, and she would make all these sounds, trying to imitate people's language. So precious she was! She was like a constant companion.

While teaching school and living in Gallup, New Mexico, I adopted a set of lovebirds. They were hand-tamed and as sweet as they could be. I would laugh as I watched them run down the hallway together. They called them lovebirds for the obvious reason; they are always making love. Their names were Jumpy for the male and Lumpy for the female. During the time I had them, they had three baby birds. To hand-tame the baby birds, they had to feed quite often. As time went on, Lumpy became pregnant again, became egg-bound, and died.

Later, I moved to Corpus Christi, Texas, and because I had to move into a smaller apartment, I gave the baby birds to a pet shop but kept Jumpy. Jumpy was an amazing bird, and he and I would take a shower together in the morning. I would often hold him in my hand, or he would sit on my shoulder. He was always giving me kisses. We made good memories together for about fifteen years. On the day he died, he stayed on my chest and didn't eat or drink all day. While on my chest, he took his final breath. It just shows you that all animals are precious and can be devoted pets to us if we invest the time to care for them.

We have a hummingbird feeder in our backyard, and those birds are pretty amazing. I especially like watching how quickly their wings move. Animals can be fascinating to watch, and I will never forget the beautiful experience of being in the water with the dolphins. Dolphins are amazing and loveable mammals. All animals are God's creatures, and they have so much love to give us. They are worth saving.

Chapter Twenty-Four: Living Your Best Life

When you connect with Mother Nature, you can have a healing experience because of all the beauty and energy surrounding you. Your senses will come alive with the sounds, smells, and visual sights you take in while in that environment. How does it feel to have the sun on your face? Or step into a cool pond or a lake?

I had a boyfriend for about five years, and we spent many weekends driving 3 1/2 hours from Massachusetts to Maine to a beautiful place called Parker Pond. Mind you, this location was out in the boonies. It rains quite often up there, but it was beautiful beyond words when it was not raining. In the mornings on the lake, you would hear the loons calling and an occasional motor from a boat. The water was calm, peaceful, and gorgeous. We would spend a lot of time water skiing during the summer months. While outdoors, we breathe in the fresh air and smell the pine trees. It was always so peaceful.

I have always been the happiest by the water and always got a rush when I was by the ocean. Have you ever seen snow in the ocean? It is quite a remarkable sight. I have always loved the sounds of the waves crashing on the shore, the smell of the fish and the salt air, and the screeching sounds of the seagulls.

My stepdad used to take us deep-sea fishing. It was always exhilarating catching those fish. One time, while on the fishing boat thirty miles from New Hampshire, we saw a giant whale. It was the size of a large building, and I was mesmerized watching it. All I could think was, "Hey, whale, don't come too close, or you'll knock our boat over into the water, and we'll probably all drown!" It was an awesome sight to see that whale. I will always feel very privileged to have witnessed seeing that whale.

We watched the pelicans dive into the water when I lived in Corpus Christi, Texas. They, too, were incredible. They would dive from incredible heights at magnificent speed above the water straight down into it. They have the most magnificent birds to look at on the Gulf Coast.

What impressed me most, though, were the dolphins. They would swim through the water with such grace and were so beautiful. They would swim by the boats as though they were guiding them out to sea. One time, my son and I went down to Cozumel, Mexico. For a birthday gift, my son arranged for him and me to get into the water with the dolphins. Such a wonderful experience with such loveable creatures. While in the water with the dolphins, they would dance with us, kiss us, and perform these incredible, unbelievable acts. They were comfortable being around people, and they trusted us. It was an experience to behold.

Yes, I will always have a place in my heart and soul for the ocean, nature, and all the beautiful creatures that come from there.

When I lived in Albuquerque, we could look out the window at the mountains. They were beautiful, and sometimes, they were snowcapped. I believe everywhere in the world has its own beauty.

When I was a small child, one of my best memories of my dad was taking my sister and me out blueberry picking. There are plenty of woods in New England, and there are lots of lakes and breathtaking beauty. Sometimes, a winter landscape can be quite awesome when the snow is white and pure or when it is falling. New England in the fall months is especially beautiful when the leaves from the trees show off their colors. Ranging from yellow to orange to red! Whenever I plan a trip back to Boston, it is always in September when the weather is perfect; it does not rain as much, it is not too hot, and it is not too cold; it is just wonderful!

It amazes me to watch how a plant will grow! From a tiny seed, then forming roots, and then transforming into a beautiful flower. Isn't nature truly fascinating? I think it's important to get outside and experience nature as much as possible. Even if it means just going to a park and feeling the beautiful grass of Mother Earth beneath your feet.

Another good memory I have of my dad was when I was a child; he would take us to a park with a pond where we fed the ducks. Spending time in nature with those you love is precious beyond words. I would like to think that the kids go outside and play instead of staying in the house glued to their computers, television, or phones all day.

When I was a child growing up near Boston, I never spent time in the house unless the weather was bad. I had friends, and we played outside. In the summertime, we would go roller skating, bicycle riding, swimming, or walking. In the wintertime, we would go sledding down the hills or ice skating on a frozen pond behind our apartment. We never stayed inside because staying inside meant cleaning the house or being disciplined. I wanted to be a free spirit, and being outside gave me that freedom.

When I was about fifteen, my girlfriend and I would walk, ride a bus, or take the subway into Boston and just look at everything. There was so much to see. There were stores to go into, and they were loaded with all kinds of merchandise to look at. There were parks to walk through and swan boats to watch. I loved the ability to walk everywhere.

One of my favorite memories is when I was about 15 or 16. My girlfriend and I went into Boston and went to the Tremont Tearoom. For the cost of $2.50, we had a sandwich of our choice and a cup of tea with tea leaves in it. We ate sandwiches and drank tea. When we finished our tea, a psychic came out and read our tea leaves, telling us about our future, and it was a neat experience. That tearoom is still there and has been since 1938! Unfortunately, they do not have the sandwiches and tea leaf readings for $2.50.

After graduating high school, I moved to Boston and attended art school. Again, I enjoyed walking through the city and always felt safe. I always knew my angels were with me to guide and protect me. But it was always important to me occasionally to get out of the city and see the country. The country will always help you best in connecting you to Mother Earth.

You can always connect by hugging those beautiful trees that surround you, whether you are in the country or the city. Ever notice how the earth always smells so fresh after a rain shower? Sometimes, you may be lucky to see a rainbow in the sky.

I feel if one stays in the house too long, they can get depressed. Going outside and connecting with nature and people will help alleviate depression and give you a sense of well-being. It may restore your health as well. God gave us this beautiful world to appreciate and enjoy each day. Give nature a chance to heal you. Be responsible for your life and live the best life possible.

Chapter Twenty-Five: How to Live a Meaningful Life
Make Peace with Your Past

Let go of grudges and forgive the past, the people, and the situations. My mother did not have an easy life. She grew up in a very wealthy town, Lincoln, Massachusetts, on the wrong side of the track. My mother developed diabetes between the ages of 11 and 12. At that time, diabetes was not a manageable disease to manage. To make matters worse, her mother died when she was 13 years old. My mother then went to live with her brother and his wife.

In her early twenties, she married my dad. My dad's parents were proud people and arrived in Boston from Nova Scotia, Canada. They were not wealthy but a bit on the snobbish side anyway. They worked hard to have the best of everything. My great-grandmother worked in a clothing store, so my grandmother always dressed well despite never going anywhere. When my mother married into the family, they made her feel inferior and not good enough for their son, but the love grew between them in time.

When I was 10 years old, my dad was extremely sick. We did not know what was wrong with him, but he stayed in bed for six months and was in a great deal of pain. He was in and out of two different hospitals, and when he was in the third one, he died. He died of a bleeding ulcer that was discovered when he had an autopsy.

Six months before he died, my dad also became diabetic. Because my mother was diabetic, she would go for regular medical appointments at Joslin Clinic at the New England Deaconess Hospital in Boston. Because my mother was also desperate to find a cure for this debilitating disease, she agreed to have my sister and I tested on a regular basis.

My sister was six years old, and I was 10 years old at the time. This meant that we would be guinea pigs for several years, subjected to hours of blood tests. Every six months, my mother would take us to the Joslin Clinic in Boston, and we would be subjected to hours of testing. One of the tests was having dye injected into us, and we would sit for hours while they watched how the dye traveled through our veins.

We had biopsies taken from various parts of our bodies and examined. One time, we had a surgical procedure where they took biopsies of our kidneys and tested the samples for diabetes. I still have an ugly, long scar from that surgery. They compared the results of our biopsies from normal people's kidneys as well as diabetic people's kidneys. There were no differences between our kidneys and people's kidneys that had no diabetes in their families. We were subjected to these tests for many years, all in the hope of a cure for diabetes. When I moved to Boston to attend college at 18, I no longer went for testing. It was very painful to subject myself to these tests. I certainly would not subject my children to this type of torture.

But this was the past, and I feel I have made peace with it. We all have memories of our past that we need to forgive so we can move on. I am sure all those involved at the clinic, including my mother, thought they were doing the right thing for the sake of science.

Stay Interested In the World Around You

Keep your life interesting and be willing to learn new things. Be curious about the world around you.

One nice thing about being in college is that you are exposed to many different subjects. As much as they are all different subjects, they all connect in some way.

The electives were fun. I remember taking horseback riding. I was a complete disaster; I was a nervous wreck, and I never felt relaxed on the top of that horse. I discovered that one of the last things I wanted to do would be to spend my time riding a horse again. But it was something new, and I learned from that experience. It widened my horizons, as well as giving me an opportunity that I might not have had.

In college, I also took jewelry-making and weaving classes. Even though I was studying to be an art teacher, neither of these classes was my strong suit. In jewelry class, I broke many metal files, and in weaving, I got all knotted up.

I took other classes such as wilderness experience, self-defense, archaeology, and many other classes that were so interesting to me. It is good to try new things; some things you would never want to do again, while others you would want to do more of. Life is interesting, and there are always things to learn. It is impossible to learn everything in one lifetime. Perhaps you would like to take a class and learn something new. There is an entire world out there ready for you to discover and explore.

Have a Good Support System

It is important to have a good support system, whether it be with friends or family.

Getting away from dysfunctional people, relationships, or partnerships is also important. If there are people you cannot get away from, such as coworkers or family, set boundaries with them and spend as little time as possible around them. You do not need to absorb that negativity.

People can only give you what they have; if they are full of love and positive energy, they will give to you. But if they are full of anger, resentment, and negativity, then that is what they will give you.

Do not allow people to humiliate you or treat you like you are beneath them. No one is better than anyone else.

Also, let people take care of their own issues and problems. You can be a sounding board, but you do not have to take on their stuff and let it absorb your time and energy.

Get To Know Yourself

- Pay attention to your thoughts and the words that you speak during the day.
- Laugh occasionally.
- Learn to love yourself and be your own best friend.
- Create space and time for yourself.
- Find the things that make you happy, find your passion, and find the time for these things.
- Find out what is the meaning of your life, your purpose.
- What are you grateful for, and what do you appreciate?
- Think of a happy memory or time that you had a good laugh.

- Decide to have a worry-free day once a week.
- Live and follow your truth.
- You are worthy of receiving, so open your heart and do so.
- Pay attention to your body.
- Send all your body parts lots of love and appreciation for all it does for you.
- Move around when you can.
- Be mindful of your breathing; breathing in and out slowly.
- Drink lots of water.
- Pay attention to how you feel around different environments as well as around different people.
- Trust how your body always feels.
- Choose love, not fear.
- Travel when you can and see different sites.
- Study diverse cultures.
- Try different foods.
- Across the world, we may look different and appear different. Still, people are people, and good and bad people are everywhere.

Explore the Arts, Go To:

- A movie
- A concert
- A museum
- A dance performance
- An opera
- An arts and crafts show
- A charity event
- A zoo
- Aquarium
- Spend a day at a spa
- Get a massage

If you must work, find a job you love.

Find a job you enjoy getting up and going to each day. If you are going to spend time and energy somewhere, make sure it is worth your while.

Know that God, your angels, spirit guides, and loved ones are all around you. That you are never truly alone. See the beauty in God and in all things, including yourself.

Never hesitate to ask for help from the other side. They want to help us, so communicate with them often.

Chapter Twenty-Six: Growing Up Catholic

Ever since I was a small child, I questioned everything. My mother would describe me as precocious, and I drove her crazy at times. I wanted answers to anything and everything. I had this insatiable desire and curiosity to know it all.

I grew up in the suburbs of Boston, about twenty miles west of the city. My parents were strict Catholics, and every Saturday, I went to confession. Every Sunday, I went to church and communion. Even though I went to confession on Saturdays, after leaving the confessional box, the guilty feeling would take over me again. For some reason, I just never felt truly holy or worthy enough.

At that time, songs and responses were spoken in Latin, not English. The masses lasted an hour and sometimes longer. The priest's sermons were meant to instill fear of God in us. He made sure we knew that when we died, we were either going to hell or purgatory because very few of us were worthy enough to enter the gates of heaven.

When one attended church, you were required to wear a mantilla on your head (if you were female) and carry a rosary or a missal (a prayer book containing the gospels). There was no need for Catholics to read the Bible because the gospels inside the missal interpreted everything from the Bible for us to know.

We would walk a mile to and from the church. One afternoon a week, we would attend catechism classes after school. Our studies involved memorizing the catechism, not questioning anything inside the book. Church and classes required a lot of kneeling, sitting, and genuflecting. And, of course, being quiet and attentive. Heaven help you if you get the giggles during mass.

The church was beautiful with all the statues, stained glass windows, and wooden pews. There was also a special warm feeling in the atmosphere, with the candles burning, the sounds of a bell, and the smell of incense and fresh flowers. It was the perfect place to pray, meditate, and feel the presence of God. It was a solemn atmosphere, peaceful but certainly not joyful.

I realize the Catholic Church has changed a great deal since those early days of my childhood. Now, the mass is done in English, not Latin. Now, you embrace your neighbor and shake hands with them. But, when I was growing up, we did what was expected of us and did not question it.

We were taught to be obedient, and that was it.

This book is about my personal journey to find those answers within myself. Not everyone may agree with my thoughts, ideas, and beliefs, and I honor our differences.

The world of metaphysics opened an entirely new world for me to look at and explore. It gave me a connection to God and the other side that I had not experienced before, and it made my heart soar.

It is not by coincidence or accident that we have come here to earth. We spent a long time planning out this carefully designed journey with our spiritual council beforehand. We have a purpose here. Our purpose is to grow spiritually on our path. The people we have chosen to deal with, our parents, our environment, and our culture are all part of this clever design to help us along the way. Karma may be involved, but it is a path we have chosen. This carefully thought-out plan is set in place, and it is up to us how we develop it. Hopefully, we will all find our way back to God and our true home on the other side. Thank you for taking this journey with me, and I hope this helps you in your journey!

Much love and many blessings along the way, Susan Grayson

Chapter Twenty-Seven: Relationships

All of us on earth in the physical body, must deal with relationships. These relationships can include personal ones: such as family or close friends. They can also include those not in our personal circle. And these associations would include our coworkers, our business associates, or just those we interact with daily.

In any case, relationships affect us. All those we meet have a positive reaction or a negative reaction on us as well as on them. These interactions may influence how we deal with our daily communications, feelings, or actions that we take. Why? Because we are exchanging energy with everyone we meet or interact with.

Some relationships may feel important, while others not so much. But all our relationships leave an impact on us regardless. Relationships, good or bad, help us grow. We learn from these experiences with others, and there is a reason these people come into our lives. Some of these people may stay in our lives a long time, while others stay only briefly. These relationships help mold our lives and can have a long-lasting effect on us, good, or bad. Words spoken, or actions taken, will forever remain with us and have a lasting effect on how we deal with relationships in the future.

The rest of this chapter will focus on four aspects important in a personal relationship. They are Communication, Adaptability, Growing Together and Love.

Communication

Words said can build us up in a positive way or, if negative, can tear us down and destroy us. Relationships are fragile and the following statements are suggestions to help make communication in our relationships successful and long lasting.

- Always try and see the other person's point of view.

- Be willing to say we are sorry, getting through and moving past that situation.

- Learn to really listen and try to understand your partner and what they are saying. We may need to ask questions to clarify what the true meaning is of what is being said.

- We should be willing to share our deepest darkest secrets and not feel uncomfortable or criticized.

- We should be willing to forgive and not hold on to the past to whatever may have been said or done.

- We must try our best not to criticize each other.

- We always must believe that our relationship will continue to get better and be willing to fight for this relationship to last forever; never giving up.

- It is important to always encourage each other to be the best they can be and to let them know we always believe in them.

- If there are age differences, have a good understanding of what that means and how things may look or seem different between the two of us.

- Pick your battles carefully. This argument may feel important now. However, a year from now, will it matter?

- Do not have regrets. Do not leave this world wishing there was something that we could have said or done differently.

Adaptability

While in relationships, there will always be transitions, circumstances, and changes we will need to adjust to together.

- It is important that we continue to like the person we have chosen to be with. Over the years we may lose our good looks or our physical ability to do the things we were once able to do.

- Defend your partner as well as always have their back.

- It is important to accept the other person's friends and family, but to also set boundaries with those people so they do not interfere with the relationship.

- Believe in the other person and the goals they are pursuing. You may also want to help them in achieving their goals when needed.

- Balance and complement each other often as well as keeping ourselves clean and attractive to each other.

- Always being faithful to each other.

- Be there for each other through sickness or in health.

- Have patience with each other as well as empathy and understanding.

- Sharing the responsibilities financial or otherwise. Both people must feel they are doing their part keeping the balance.

- Both of us must want this relationship to work and we will not give up on it!

Growing Together

In a relationship, it is important that we can grow together. The following are examples of how we can achieve this.

- We must have similar goals, plans, and dreams that we can develop together. We must keep those goals, plans, and dreams alive.

- It is important that we do things together, maybe even new things. It can be as simple as sitting down and having dinner together, watching a movie, or taking a walk.

- Show an interest in what our partner is doing or learning. We may have different interests and we may not want to take part in that same activity but show an interest. Let them know we care while also allowing each other to find their own path.

- Try and do new and fun things together. Maybe traveling or taking a class is something we would like to do, going to new places and experiencing new things.

- It is important that we both have the same lifestyle, are career or goal oriented, and have the same interests. That can mean raising a family or running a business together. It is important that we both know and agree with what is expected in this relationship because we are building this foundation together.

- We can see a future as one. We are like a team. We join efforts to make it work.

- Having mutual respect and that we can be selfless, thoughtful, accepting and kind to our significant person in our life.

Love

Love is all about really caring about a person and loving them unconditionally by allowing them to be themselves and being their own person. The dictionary defines love as an intense deep affection for another person. Love is also about both partners investing in each other's happiness and well-being. Below are pointers to consider about love and how to keep it alive and well.

- Love is about accepting the other person's faults, shortcomings, and moods.

- By loving the other person, we put that relationship first more than anything else. There are times in our relationship when we may have to sacrifice for the other person to make them happy.

- We must be able to see the other person as worthy, good, and knowing why we chose them in the first place. We must also believe we have the best relationship possible for us and we will stay in this relationship always, matter what happens.

- It also important to believe that our partner will always choose us and stay with us also.

- We must have intimacy in a relationship. That does not necessarily mean sex, but it does mean at least having affection between the two of you. That could be touching, hugging, holding hands, or cuddling up together.

- Occasionally, we can bring our partner home a delightful surprise gift, something they would love, it does not have to be expensive, but it must be meaningful.

- We must have a relationship where we can laugh or cry together as well as having a shoulder to lean on.

- Be there to help the other person through a demanding situation. Help them by picking up the pieces. An example of this would be like a death in the family, or some other traumatic time in their lives. It is important to be there for them.

- Letting the other person shine, giving them the spotlight.

- Being able to nurture the other person.

- In a relationship it is important to be best friends. They are the ones we wish to spend our time with, to come home to.

- Always tell them we love them. We may be upset with them or have an argument with them, but always tell them we really love them.

- It is important that we always feel loved, protected, and safe with that person.

- In our relationship, it is imperative that we love ourselves. We also must find and know who we are and who and what we want in life.

- Just because we are in a relationship, it is important that we do not lose ourselves just because we are in one.

- We must always be our own best friends. We must keep our goals and our dreams alive, our interests and passions. We should support our self-respect and do not forget who we are. We must keep our integrity and never compromise our values.

- Above all, we must continue to love ourselves, so we choose wisely. As Shakespeare said, "To thine own self be true."

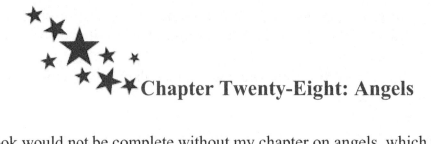# Chapter Twenty-Eight: Angels

My book would not be complete without my chapter on angels, which was channeled through me two early mornings.

Angels will rarely take on a physical body unless it requires a miracle on the physical plane. They are our closest friends, and they love us unconditionally. When we meditate or center ourselves, still our emotions, and remove our ego, it is easier to connect with them. We may ask our angels for assistance for us or for other people. They cannot interfere with our lives but will assist us when we ask them to.

Angels are benevolent beings who watch over us. They are always with us, surrounding us with their love and whispering guidance in our ears. They are always there to protect us. Our angels share our everyday experiences with us. When we are sad or cry, they feel our pain.

When we have fun and laugh, they feel our joy.

We have that special angel, our guardian angel, who has been with us since birth. They have been with us from the time we were born, and they know and understand us better than we do. The guardian angel that has been assigned to us before we were born will stay with us all our life and guide us safely to the other side into the arms of our loved ones when we pass from this world.

Our angels see all we do, the good and the bad, our loving gestures and our not-so-kind ones. They do not judge us. These spiritual beings love us unconditionally and understand us in our human form. They have compassion for us and realize the challenges we go through daily while on the physical plane.

They know we are worthy of love. Our angels see our shortcomings, and they want us to forgive ourselves. They forgive us when they see us lash out in anger because they know it is part of our human condition.

Our angels feel honored when we call upon them and request their help in any way. When we encounter a situation that we need help with, they are at our side and stay with us until our problem is solved. They will even intuitively guide us with workable solutions.

While on earth, our angels try to warn us when opportunities come and present themselves to us that will be beneficial. Sometimes, they appear to us in dreams, and we wake up knowing about something. They may give us an answer to a question we have been having.

They see our potential and try to make us aware of the fact that we are so much more than we think we are. Although we have free will in this lifetime, they occasionally will give us the guidance needed to help us stay on our spiritual path.

I believe in angels, and I know that that light within us connects us to them and to the heavens beyond.

If we see numbers repeatedly, that is the angel's way of letting us know they are with us and that we are not alone, not now, not ever.

The angels want us to live our lives fully, engage with and find satisfaction in our daily lives, and know that life truly is precious and worth living. Every day, we can find joy and happiness if we desire. Angels want us to love ourselves as they love us. They see the purity and beauty of our soul and the light within us

We will not live on earth forever, but it is important that we appreciate why we chose to come here and what we choose to learn while being here. Maybe we came here to reconnect with loved ones we have known before. Or it may be the beauty of the earth that has drawn us to this place. We were brought here because we were sent here on a mission to make a difference in the lives of people around us. Some groups of people may need our help, and we are here to show them a better life. Or a better way.

It is important to trust that there is a reason we are here; we are not here by accident or coincidence. We have a purpose on earth. While on earth, the angels will help us by sending people to us, or they may have us read an article or see a particular program on TV, but there will be signs all around us from our angels. It is up to us to be aware of those messages they send we. They will only help us if it is for our highest good. Please just know they are always with us, and find the time to communicate with them.

Angels want us to live our lives without regrets.

They want us to live each day as though it is our last. If we need to make amends about something, we should do so. Every day should be spent expressing our love for one another, our love for our planet, and our love for ourselves. We should be grateful for each day and see everything we acquire in our lifetime as gifts.

Our friendships are important. Our friendships are the people we have chosen to travel with us on this journey. Some friends will stay with us for a lifetime, while others will remain with us only briefly. But while they are in our lives, they all have something to share and teach us.

We will carry all these experiences we have had, the stories we created, and the relationships we formed with us to the other side. Nothing that we learn here on earth is forgotten. Those memories are carefully stored inside our minds. Those familiar faces we loved will remain with us, too. It is all good. We are not judged; we judge ourselves.

Because this is the physical world we are in, all our senses that were so alive on this planet will also stay with us. Whether it is the smell of our mother's perfume, our father's cigarettes, or those freshly baked pies our grandmother made, these are all part of the memories we take with us. We will also remember the smell of the land after a rain shower, our hair after it is freshly washed, the smell of the ocean, and the smell of the freshly cut flowers we placed on our table.

We will remember the people we have loved here. We will remember our joy, laughter, and the pain and tears we shared together. These precious memories we share with others will be carefully stored and never truly forgotten. The times we played with our pets, the way they always greeted us, and the sounds they made will not be forgotten.

All the beauty we have witnessed while on this plane will stay with us, the beauty of a rainbow after a storm, the green of the earth, the winds, and the sunshine on our faces, the rain, and the snow. All of this makes us feel truly alive in the physical world. All the physical sensations on earth will be etched upon our souls.

We will remember the words spoken to us, as well as the hugs and embraces. We will remember the first time we held our child, the first time we held hands with the person we were fond of, our first kiss, our first touch, and our first intimate time with another. We will remember our relationships, the joys, and the pain that comes with the heartache. It has been a journey. One of love, joy, fear, and hate. And we would not have changed it for anything because it was all part of our creation that God allowed us to bring into existence. That is why we may continue to return and make more memories with those we loved that were precious to us.

We will also remember our first accomplishments and successes and how they made we feel. The physical pain and the physical joy of endurance in accomplishing a feat we thought impossible. This is the story of our life, and it is unique, unlike anyone else's. It is what has made our life entirely ours and ours alone. Cherish it, all of it, and do not regret it one bit. We are loved for all we have done here. Our angels have loved us through all this, and they understand us. If we come back here, it will be even better next time! We have not experienced this alone because our angels have always been with us. Our angels will always love us.

Made in the USA
Middletown, DE
03 May 2024